Seeing Through Legalese

Seeing Through Legalese

More Essays on Plain Language

Joseph Kimble

For Victoria Faustin —
with thanks for
your help And
Admiration for your
Accomplishments.

Joe Kimble
October 2017

CAROLINA ACADEMIC PRESS
Durham, North Carolina

Library of Congress Cataloging-in-Publication Data

Kimble, Joseph.
    Seeing through legalese: more essays on plain language /
Joseph Kimble
                    p. cm.
    Includes bibliographical references and index.
    ISBN 978-1-53100-864-2 (alk. paper)
    1. Legal composition. 2. Law — United States — Language.
2. Law — United States — Terminology.

KF250 .K534 2017
808.06/634—dc23   2017037660

Carolina Academic Press
700 Kent Street
Durham, North Carolina 27701
Telephone (919) 489-7486
Fax (919) 493-5668
www.cap-press.com

Printed in the United States of America

To all my students, for their commitment during my three decades of teaching at Western Michigan University–Thomas Cooley Law School. And to all the school's librarians, for never failing to deliver.

CONTENTS

PART TWO: ON LEGAL WRITING GENERALLY

PART THREE: INTERVIEWS AND REMARKS

PREFACE

This is my third — and possibly my last — book on legal writing. In recent years, I've been writing mainly about legal interpretation. While I plan to continue that pursuit, I'll no doubt still keep plugging away at the good fight for clear, plain legal writing, my life's work.

The first book, *Lifting the Fog of Legalese: Essays on Plain Language*, collected articles and shorter pieces I had written up until about 2006. In the Introduction, I said what I have to say about the general state of legal writing — and concluded like this (page xv):

> Such a mess we lawyers have gotten ourselves into. And because law touches almost everything in some way, so does the fog of legalese. I think no reform would more fundamentally improve our profession and the work we do than learning to express ourselves in plain language.

In the second book, *Writing for Dollars, Writing to Please: The Case for Plain Language in Business, Government, and Law*, I listed 40 or so elements of plain language, addressed 10 false criticisms, described 40 historical highlights in the push for reform, and summarized 50 empirical case studies showing the extraordinary benefits of using plain language in legal and official writing. My emphasis, as expressed in the subtitle, was on the foundations of plain language and not on how to practice it.

Now this third book, collecting essays since 2006 and returning to a mix of guidance, rebuttal, and reflection. Have things improved in the last decade, or indeed in the last 30 years? I think so. But nobody knows for sure, because how could you even begin to assess the great mass of legal writing and drafting then and now? And in any event, gains will always be incremental in a profession as tied to tradition as law.

So forget the revolution. Just know that more forces are at work for better legal writing than ever before — in the law schools, in the literature, in the CLE courses, in various pockets of government, and in multiple organizations and groups worldwide. No revolution; just a gradual cutting down and cleaning up of one verbose pile after another, until readers can see more easily through the legalese — to the light of clarity.

A few words about these essays.

Much of the practical benefit will come from close attention to the examples, the side-by-side comparisons, and my comments on the differences. I realize that some of the boxed columns are narrow and that some of the comments (especially the footnotes on pages 98–123) are extensive, but I'm confident that they will repay study.

The technical bane of all scholarly writers these days is ever-changing URLs. I honestly thought about omitting them entirely and just telling readers to Google the cited sources. I decided against that, but I'll give readers the same advice as a backup: if a URL fails, Google the author and title. All three were last checked in August 2017.

Finally, although I've tweaked and updated many of the essays, each one appears almost as it did originally. If this makes for a little repetition, so be it. Let's just say that those points were especially important.

I hope you enjoy this collection, learn some things, nod in agreement often, and even smile from time to time.

I am indebted to so many people.

First, the group of readers who regularly agree to comment on new work and invariably sharpen it: Mark Cooney, Thomas Myers, Laurel Romanella, and MaryAnn Pierce.

Then those people who kindly reviewed at least one of these essays: Judge Lee Rosenthal, Bryan Garner, Joseph Spaniol, David Schultz, Fred Baker, Jery Payne, Annetta Cheek, Christopher Balmford, Ross Guberman, and Ginny Redish.

Then my long-suffering assistant, Cindy Hurst, who first typeset all the essays. And Linda Novak, the patient and proficient editor of the *Michigan Bar Journal*, where many of the essays first appeared. (See the acknowledgments on page 247.)

Finally, Karen Magnuson, who copyedits just about everything I write, including the two previous books. She is the best.

To all of you, my deep and abiding thanks.

PART ONE

On Legal Drafting

You Think Lawyers Are Good Drafters?

No, I'm sorry, but most lawyers are not skilled drafters. It doesn't matter how smart or experienced they are or how many legal documents they have drafted. Most — a supermajority, probably — are lacking. And yet, oddly enough, while they tend to be blind to their own shortcomings, the poor quality of others' drafting is plain for them to see.[1] When was the last time you heard a lawyer praise the clarity of a statute or rule or contract?

Elsewhere, I've identified five reasons for this professional deficiency,[2] but I think two of them stand out. First, until recently, law schools have tended to neglect legal drafting. Shamefully neglect. For how can lawyers practice effectively without training in how to draft — and critically review — legal instruments? Second, rather than take it upon themselves to acquire the skill, lawyers naturally turn to formbooks — those bastions of dense, verbose, antiquated drafting. So the ineptitude cycles on.

Neglect by law schools. The poor models in formbooks. If anything, law schools have historically provided a perverse kind of antitraining — through the models that the profession itself saddled them with. Think of the generations of law students who studied, intensively, the Internal Revenue Code, the Uniform Commercial Code, the Federal Rules of Civil Procedure, and the Federal Rules of Evidence, among

---

[1] *See* Bryan A. Garner, *President's Letter*, The Scrivener 1, 3 (Winter 1998) (reporting on the author's survey of lawyers at his seminars: they view only 5% of the documents they read as well drafted, but amazingly, 95% would claim that they draft high-quality documents).

[2] *See* this book at 57–59.

other such promulgations. And I doubt that many professors made it a point to criticize the drafting in those laws and
rules or occasionally asked the class to work on improving a
provision. So most law students must have come away with
the impression that the drafting was perfectly normal and
generally good. Well, it may have been normal, but it was
far from good, as I've tried to show.[3] The heartening news is
that current and future generations will at least not have to
endure the old Federal Rules of Civil Procedure and Rules
of Evidence, since completely redrafted sets took effect in
2007 and 2011.

Still, we need to be constantly reminded of how pervasive the ailment is in our profession, so I'll dutifully keep
nagging.

Another Would-Be Model

In October 2012, the Charleston School of Law hosted
a symposium on Federal Rule of Evidence 502 — governing
the extent to which a waiver occurs when a party discloses
legally protected information. As part of the symposium,
the participating judges, lawyers, and professors prepared a
"model" order to carry out Rule 502(d), which allows a judge
to order that a disclosure connected with pending litigation
does not create a waiver. The order was published in the
Fordham Law Review,[4] and it presumably has, or will, come
to the attention of federal district judges. Thus, another typical piece of drafting makes the rounds as an imitable form, an
example to follow, a convenient resource.

At the end of this article, I have reproduced the order as
published. (On a positive note, the word *shall* is nowhere to
be found.) Alongside it is my redraft. I'll first highlight the

---

[3]   *See* this book at 35–126.
[4]   Symposium Participants, *Model Draft of a Rule 502(d) Order*, 81 Fordham
      L. Rev. 1587 (2013).

drafting slips in the original and then stand on the comparison between the two versions.

So what's wrong?

- The original uses 125 more words than the revision.

- The first sentence favors us with hardcore legalese — *pursuant to*.

- The original uses four unnecessary parenthetical definitions (starting with "Disclosing Party"). This is one of the worst tics of all — producing any number of distracting, unnecessary capitals.

- In several places, the original departs from the language of Rule 502 for no apparent reason. For instance, section (a) uses *waiver or forfeiture*, but *forfeiture* does not appear in 502. And then (b) drops *forfeiture*, creating further inconsistency. For another instance, (a) refers to information that is *privileged* — generally — or *protected by the attorney-client privilege*. But 502 refers to the latter only. Why the difference?

- The sequence of events seems questionable. Under (b), the receiving party must — unless it contests the claimed privilege or protection — notify the disclosing party that the receiving party will make best efforts to properly handle the information. Then the disclosing party has five business days to explain its claim. But can the receiving party usually know whether to contest the claim before getting the explanation? My redraft follows the sequencing in the original, but should the disclosing party's explanation (my (d)) accompany its original notification (my (b))?

- The second sentence in (a) is 94 words. The average sentence length in the original is 34 words. The revised version averages 26.

- The second sentence begins with the truism *Subject to the provisions of this Order*. And note the pointless (and inconsistent) capitalization of *order*.

- Besides *pursuant to*, (a) contains two other multi-word prepositions — *in connection with* and *with respect to*.

- (b) and (f) both contain unnecessary cross-references.

- (b) should be divided into additional sections.

- (b) uses *review, dissemination, and use*, but (e) uses *examining or disclosing* for what seem to be the same ideas.

- (e) and (g) start with *Nothing in this order*, but (h) doesn't follow suit.

- (e) uses *privileged* only, not *privileged or protected*. Is that difference intended?

- (f) switches from *Proving* in the heading to *establishing* in the text. What's the difference?

- The relationship between the two sentences in (h) needs clarifying, but I didn't venture into that.

- After the first mention, *attorney-client privilege or work product protection* can be shortened to *privilege or protection*. That's what Rule 502 does.

- *Work-product protection* needs a hyphen throughout.

Incidentally, if my revision makes some inadvertent substantive change, it would be easy to fix and would hardly rationalize the old-style drafting in the original.

One more time: legal drafting is a demanding skill that needs to be learned and practiced. The more important the project, and the more it affects the public or the profession, then the more important it is that this skill shine through.

[A side-by-side comparison begins on the next page.]

MODEL DRAFT OF A RULE 502(d) ORDER	REVISED DRAFT
(a) No Waiver by Disclosure. This order is entered pursuant to Rule 502(d) of the Federal Rules of Evidence. Subject to the provisions of this Order, if a party (the "Disclosing Party") discloses information in connection with the pending litigation that the Disclosing Party thereafter claims to be privileged or protected by the attorney-client privilege or work product protection ("Protected Information"), the disclosure of that Protected Information will not constitute or be deemed a waiver or forfeiture — in this or any other action — of any claim of privilege or work product protection that the Disclosing Party would otherwise be entitled to assert with respect to the Protected Information and its subject matter.	**(a) No Waiver by Disclosure.** This order is entered under Federal Rule of Evidence 502(d). It applies when a party discloses information connected with this litigation and later claims that the information is covered by the attorney–client privilege or work-product protection. By disclosing, the party does not waive — in this action or any other — any claim of privilege or protection concerning the information or its subject matter.
(b) Notification Requirements; Best Efforts of Receiving Party. A Disclosing Party must promptly notify the party receiving the Protected Information ("the Receiving	**(b) Giving Notice of the Disclosing Party's Claim.** The disclosing party must, in writing, promptly notify the party receiving the information that it is privileged or

Party"), in writing, that it has disclosed that Protected Information without intending a waiver by the disclosure. Upon such notification, the Receiving Party must — unless it contests the claim of attorney-client privilege or work product protection in accordance with paragraph (c) — promptly (i) notify the Disclosing Party that it will make best efforts to identify and return, sequester or destroy (or in the case of electronically stored information, delete) the Protected Information and any reasonably accessible copies it has and (ii) provide a certification that it will cease further review, dissemination, and use of the Protected Information. Within five business days of receipt of the notification from the Receiving Party, the Disclosing Party must explain as specifically as possible why the Protected Information is privileged. [For purposes of this Order, Protected Information that has been stored on a source of electronically stored information that is not reasonably accessible, such as backup storage media, is sequestered. If such data is retrieved, the Receiving Party must promptly take steps to delete or sequester the restored protected information.]

protected and that no waiver is intended.

(c) **Action by the Receiving Party if It Does Not Contest the Claim.** Upon receiving notice, the receiving party must promptly do the following unless it contests the claim: (1) notify the disclosing party that it will make its best efforts to identify and to return, sequester, or destroy (or electronically delete) the information and any reasonably accessible copies it has; and (2) certify that it will not further review, disseminate, or use the information. [The information is sequestered if stored on an electronic source that is not reasonably accessible. If the information is retrieved, the receiving party must promptly take steps to sequester or delete it.]

(d) **Explanation by the Disclosing Party.** Within five business days after receiving the best-efforts notice in (c), the disclosing party must explain as specifically as possible why the information is privileged or protected. [*Should the explanation accompany the notice in (b)?*]

(c) Contesting Claim of Privilege or Work Product Protection. If the Receiving Party contests the claim of attorney-client privilege or work product protection, the Receiving Party must — within five business days of receipt of the notice of disclosure — move the Court for an Order compelling disclosure of the information claimed as unprotected (a "Disclosure Motion"). The Disclosure Motion must be filed under seal and must not assert as a ground for compelling disclosure the fact or circumstances of the disclosure. Pending resolution of the Disclosure Motion, the Receiving Party must not use the challenged information in any way or disclose it to any person other than those required by law to be served with a copy of the sealed Disclosure Motion.

(d) Stipulated Time Periods. The parties may stipulate to extend the time periods set forth in paragraphs (b) and (c).

(e) Attorney's Ethical Responsibilities. Nothing in this order overrides any attorney's ethical

(e) Contesting the Claim. If the receiving party contests the claim of privilege or protection, then within five business days after receiving notice of the claim, the receiving party must move for an order compelling disclosure of all or part of the information. The motion must be filed under seal and must not assert as one of its grounds the facts or circumstances of the disclosure. While the motion is pending, the receiving party must not use the challenged information in any way or disclose it to anyone except those who are legally required to be served with the motion.

(f) Stipulating to a Different Time Period. The parties may stipulate to extend the time periods in (d) and (e).

(g) Burden of Proving Privilege or Protection. The disclosing party has the burden of proving a contested claim of privilege or protection.

(h) Attorney's Ethical Responsibilities. This order does not override an attorney's responsibilities to refrain from examining or disclosing materials that the attorney knows or reasonably should know to be privileged and to inform the Disclosing Party that such materials have been produced.

ethical responsibility to (1) refrain from reviewing, disseminating, or using materials that the attorney knows or reasonably should know to be privileged and (2) inform the disclosing party that those materials have been produced.

(f) Burden of Proving Privilege or Work-Product Protection. The Disclosing Party retains the burden — upon challenge pursuant to paragraph (c) — of establishing the privileged or protected nature of the Protected Information.

(g) In camera Review. Nothing in this Order limits the right of any party to petition the Court for an *in camera* review of the Protected Information.

(i) In Camera Review. This order does not limit a party's right to petition the court to review the information in camera.

(h) Voluntary and Subject Matter Waiver. This Order does not preclude a party from voluntarily waiving the attorney-client privilege or work product protection. The provisions of Federal Rule 502(a) apply when the Disclosing Party uses or indicates that it may use information produced under this Order to support a claim or defense.

(j) Voluntary and Subject-Matter Waiver. This order does not preclude a party from voluntarily waiving the attorney–client privilege or work-product protection. Federal Rule of Evidence 502(a) applies when the disclosing party uses or indicates that it may use information produced under this order to support a claim or defense.

(i) Rule 502(b)(2). The provisions of Federal Rule of Evidence 502(b)(2) are inapplicable to the production of Protected Information under this Order.

(k) Inapplicability of Rule 502(b)(2). Federal Rule of Evidence 502(b)(2) does not apply to producing information under this order.

You Think the Law Requires Legalese?

There's a sign that, in some configuration, appears on every gas pump in Michigan, although most drivers probably don't even notice it anymore. Here's a photo of one:

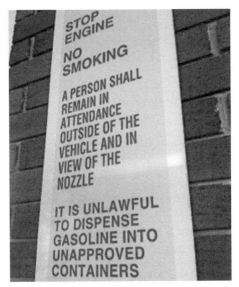

Let's put aside the all-capitals, which are notoriously hard to read. And never mind that the first and second items aren't exactly parallel. ("Stop engine. Don't smoke.") The trouble — linguistically, stylistically, semantically — shows up in the third item.

Look at that little sentence. We get an explicit subject, *A person*, which really throws off the parallelism. The lawyer's *shall* — now corrupted and ambiguous from misuse — does not belong even in statutes or regulations, let alone on a gas pump. *Remain in attendance*? Oh, please. The first *of* is unnecessary. And for the big comedic finish, we're seemingly told that the nozzle must be able to see the person.

The fix isn't hard: "You must stay outside your vehicle and be able to see the nozzle." Or for parallelism with the first two items: "Stay outside your vehicle, and make sure you can see the nozzle."

Now, are people likely to misunderstand the pump version? No. Is this the worst public writing on the planet? Obviously not. But by tracing this mundane example to its source, anyone who cares about clarity in legal and official documents can learn a set of critical lessons.

The Limited Force of Statutes and Regulations

Our gas-pump example has its origins in a Michigan regulation, Mich. Admin. Code R. 29.5325, § 9.2.5.4:

> Warning signs shall be conspicuously posted in the dispensing area and shall incorporate the following **or equivalent** wording: "WARNING. It is unlawful and dangerous to dispense gasoline into unapproved containers. No smoking. Stop motor. No filling of portable containers in or on a motor vehicle. The person shall remain in attendance outside of the vehicle and in view of the nozzle."

The order of the items here is different from our sign, there's an additional item about not filling portable containers, and a few words have changed — probably because the regulation has been amended over time. But that doesn't matter. The point is that the sign essentially uses the regulatory language — even though it didn't have to. Note the language that I bolded above: the gas station could have used something *equivalent* to "A person shall remain in attendance outside of the vehicle and in view of the nozzle." The station could have written it simpler and shorter.

Now imagine a scenario, however unlikely, between some inquisitive station owner and an attorney for the Michigan Petroleum Association:

Owner: You know those signs we have to have on our pumps — about not smoking and standing outside when somebody pumps gas?

Attorney: Yup. You mean those standard warning signs that everybody buys from Signs-R-Us?

Owner: Right. The other day, some customer was jagging me about the weird language — nozzles with eyes, or something.

Attorney: Well, it may be weird, but it's required by law. No choice. I think there's a state regulation that spells it out.

Owner: Wouldn't you know? Okay. Just wondering. I certainly wasn't going to order a new sign. Good thing the grammar police aren't licensed to give tickets.

This scenario has never happened and never will. But a variation on it happens all the time. I hear about it regularly from colleagues involved in plain language, I read about it, I've experienced it myself, and I've written about one typical instance — a project "derailed" by the legal team of New York City's Department of Transportation because the revision "did not use the same legal language as the original."[1] All too often, legal departments either mistake what the law requires or can't be bothered with matters of "mere style."

And there's a third impediment to clarity that falls somewhere in between: lawyers' reluctance to depart from statutory or regulatory language even when they know they can. That is, even those lawyers who are generally receptive to plain language may balk when they perceive that statutes or regulations are hovering around. For instance, one

---

[1] Joseph Kimble, *Writing for Dollars, Writing to Please: The Case for Plain Language in Business, Government, and Law* 34 (2012).

blemish on the restyled Federal Rules of Criminal Procedure is the repeated use of *the attorney for the government*
instead of *the government attorney*. Why? Because federal
statutes use the former. As if there were the slightest risk
in changing . . . At one point during the restyling of the
Civil Rules, I changed *Acts of Congress* to *federal statutes*
(for consistency with other rules, no less), and an influential
voice commented: "Although 28 U.S.C. § 2071 says 'Acts of
Congress,' I will give you this one without protest." What
a concession. If you want one setting where this attitude
would be a disaster, look no further than jury instructions.[2]

I don't mean to suggest that the language of statutes
and regulations is never mandatory. Michigan's Landlord–
Tenant Relationship Act requires that the parties complete
an inventory checklist, which "shall contain the following
notice."[3] There's no getting around the language that appears
in quotes after *notice*.

But I'm willing to bet, without having done any kind of
survey, that it would turn up at least as many statutes and
regulations with language like this:

- *shall incorporate the following or equivalent language*
  (our gas-pump regulation)
- *shall state . . . a notice in substantially the following
  form*[4]
- *The statement shall be in a form similar to the following*[5]
- a *statement substantially similar to Model Form G–4*[6]

---

[2]   *See* Joseph Kimble, *How to Mangle Court Rules and Jury Instructions*, in
      Lifting the Fog of Legalese: Essays on Plain Language 105, 115–16 (2006)
      (giving examples of statutes converted to plain jury instructions).
[3]   Mich. Comp. Laws Ann. § 554.608(4).
[4]   *Id.* § 554.634(2).
[5]   21 C.F.R. § 1304.40(b)(2).
[6]   12 C.F.R. § 226.9(a)(2).

- *a written notice containing all of the following information[7]*
- *a statement specifying that*
- *shall contain language that[8]*

None of these formulations says to "use these words."

So what are the lessons to be drawn from all this? They number five. First, codified language will often get copied or at least cause second-guessing — so draft in plain language to begin with. Second, lawyers tend to greatly exaggerate the extent to which the law requires specific, unalterable wording in legal and official documents. Third, if you're told that certain unplain language is legally necessary, you should kindly ask for a citation, a reference. (Nonlawyers, do it!) Fourth, if you don't get one, the lawyer is either at a loss or indifferent. Finally, if you do get one, check it out. Nonlawyers can usually get any needed help from law-school or university libraries. And when you find the cited law, look for the kind of language in the bullet points above — meaning that legalese is not required.

The Minimal and Manageable Force of Terms of Art

Another potent myth, or half-truth, or quarter-truth, commonly invades any discussion of legal writing: lawyers must use terms of art. Woe is them. Their hands are tied.

Once again, much exaggerated. I'll just briefly review points I've made elsewhere.

Even if we take the broad view that any term ever litigated is a term of art, they would count for a tiny part of most legal documents. (Obviously, this view is overinclusive: the term *herein* has been litigated many times, and it's hardly

---

[7] Mich. Comp. Laws Ann. § 339.918(1).

[8] *Id.* § 339.2515(1).

a term of art.) In one empirical study using a real-estate sales contract, researchers found that less than 3% of the words had significant legal meaning based on precedent.[9]

Now consider the tiny fraction of words that *have* been litigated. Can we say that they have been honed by precedent and are thus irreplaceable? That question prompts others. How many cases does it take before a term is well honed? Why couldn't we conclude that the more times a term has been litigated, the more troublesome it is? What do we do about inconsistent interpretations? Do drafters generally operate more from considered, thoughtful choice or from habit and imitation?

At any rate, we again have research that helps inform this discussion. In 1995, the Centre for Plain Legal Language at Sydney University's Faculty of Law published *Law Words: 30 Essays on Legal Words & Phrases*.[10] As the title suggests, the contributors carefully researched 30 terms that many lawyers would classify as terms of art. And for almost every one, the research showed that the term was unnecessary, troublesome, best used together with a plainer term, or replaceable with a plain equivalent. For example: *give*, not *give, devise, and bequeath*; *interest*, not *right, title, and interest*; *together and individually*, not *jointly and severally*. Surely, research in the U.S. on these terms — and many more that we might pluck from *Words & Phrases* — would produce the same conclusions about their value and need in this country.

In fact, to take another example, how about the word *indemnify*? Isn't that a term of art — if anything is? Well, check out the Plain Language column in the September 2013 *Michigan Bar Journal*.[11] A seasoned commercial lawyer says otherwise: it can be replaced with *pay for*. More recently, he

---

[9] Benson Barr et al., *Legalese and the Myth of Case Precedent*, 64 Mich. B.J. 1136, 1137 (Oct. 1985).

[10] http://www.clarity-international.net/documents/law_words.pdf.

[11] Jeffrey S. Ammon, Indemnification: *Banish the Word! And Rebuild Your Indemnity Clause from Scratch*, Mich. B.J., Sept. 2013, at 52.

suggested ditching another supposed term of art — *time is of the essence* — which he criticized as unclear, misleading, and inadequate.[12]

One other point, about consumer documents, especially. If you're uncomfortable with abandoning the traditional term entirely, you can usually still find a way to pair it with plain words or an explanation the first time you use it: "attached items (called 'fixtures')"; "I release, or give up, any legal claims"; "a default judgment — which means that the court will give the plaintiff what he is asking for." Then try to stick with the plain term in any later uses. And don't be surprised if readers sing your praises for helping them understand.[13]

Terms of art are more rare and more replaceable than we lawyers like to think. Even a cautious drafter requires only an occasional legal term, which need not stand alone, unclarified. All the other principles and techniques of plain language can still be brought to bear.[14]

The law is no serious obstacle to writing clearly and plainly.

---

[12] Jeffrey S. Ammon, Time Is of the Essence *(to Banish That Phrase from Your Contracts)!*, Mich. B.J., Feb. 2016, at 40; *see also* Chadwick C. Busk & Michael Braem, *Curiouser & Curiouser Excuses for Legal Jargon*, Mich. B.J., Oct. 2016, at 30, 34 (arguing that just because you can find a case that applied a time-is-of-the-essence clause doesn't mean that a clause "drafted in plain language wouldn't have accomplished the same result").

[13] *See* Christopher R. Trudeau, *The Public Speaks: An Empirical Study of Legal Communication*, 14 Scribes J. Legal Writing 121, 149–50 (2011–2012) (reporting on a survey in which, for one question, the public overwhelmingly preferred that legal terms be accompanied by an explanation).

[14] *See* Kimble, *Writing for Dollars, Writing to Please* at 5–10 (listing more than 40 guidelines).

Guiding Principles for Restyling the Federal Rules of Civil Procedure

I wrote this memorandum as drafting consultant on the project to restyle the Federal Rules of Civil Procedure. The memo accompanied the restyled rules when they were published for comment, side by side with the then-current rules, in February 2005. Those two versions are still available by searching Google for this report: "Advisory Committee on Rules of Civil Procedure, December 2004." The new rules took effect in December 2007. Of course, some of them may have changed since then.

This memorandum is meant to introduce readers to the restyled Federal Rules of Civil Procedure. It briefly describes the process for producing the restyled rules and then highlights some of the main style considerations and constraints.

The Style Process

This project was a style project, and the Advisory Committee on Civil Rules took extraordinary steps to avoid making any substantive changes. Here is an outline of those steps.

First, the style consultants prepared an original working draft — the redraft of the current rules.

Second, the Committee's reporter, along with one of two other experts on civil procedure, reviewed the draft in detailed memorandums that identified possible changes in meaning.

Third, the style consultants revised the original draft in light of the experts' comments. This produced draft #2, which footnoted any outstanding issues.

Fourth, draft #2 was submitted to the style subcommittee of the Standing Committee on Rules of Practice and Procedure, which itself included an academic expert on civil procedure. The style subcommittee reviewed the entire draft, including the outstanding issues. The style subcommittee resolved many of the issues but decided that some were better resolved by the Advisory Committee. The style subcommittee's work resulted in draft #3. The reporter footnoted draft #3 for review by the Advisory Committee.

Fifth, the Advisory Committee broke down into Subcommittees A and B, each of which reviewed half the rules. If a "significant minority" of Subcommittee A or B thought that certain wording created a substantive change, then the wording was not approved. One of two representatives of the ABA's Litigation Section submitted comments on the drafts, attended each subcommittee meeting, and participated in the discussion. The work of the subcommittees resulted in draft #4.

Sixth, the full Advisory Committee reviewed the work of the subcommittees, concentrating on issues that the subcommittees thought should be resolved by the full Committee. This resulted in draft #5, the final draft.

Seventh, the restyled rules were reviewed by the Standing Committee — and changed in response to its suggestions — as each set of rules was produced.

This process took two and a half years and produced more than 600 documents. Anyone who reviews this archive will realize how much time and care and expertise were involved in preparing the restyled rules. The Committee's watchword appears in every Committee Note: "These changes are intended to be stylistic only." Everything that applied before this style project applies after the project.

Style Matters

In General

At the outset, the Advisory Committee adopted these authoritative guides on drafting and style: for drafting, Bryan Garner's *Guidelines for Drafting and Editing Court Rules*; for usage and style, Garner's *Dictionary of Modern Legal Usage* (2d ed. 1995) [3d ed. published 2011]; for spelling, *Merriam-Webster's Collegiate Dictionary* (11th ed. 2003). These sources will explain many of the Committee's decisions — everything from starting sentences with *But* to the use of hyphens and dashes to the preference for verbs rather than abstract nouns (*serve*, not *effect service*; *sued*, not *brought suit*).

Of course, it's difficult to even begin to describe the myriad style questions that arose during the project. The Committee developed a chart of more than 50 so-called global, or recurring, issues (*allege* or *aver*? *issue an order* or *make an order*?). Then there were the individual style questions — the possible edits — that every sentence, clause, and phrase in the rules seemed to present. Start with the first sentence of the rules. Should it be *all suits of a civil nature*? No: *all civil actions*. Should it be *with the exceptions stated in Rule 81*? No: *except as stated in Rule 81*. And so on, sentence by sentence.

Readers will notice, as they compare the rules side by side, that the restyled rules are usually shorter and easier to read. Some of the restyled rules may look longer on the page only because of the formatting — the breakdown into subparts and lists. Take Rule 9(a). The current rule is 127 words of text; the restyled rule is 78 words.

This is not to say that the project's goal was to cut words; that was a natural result of the effort to clarify and simplify. Here are just two short examples:

Rule 8(e)(2)

When two or more statements are made in the alternative and one of them if made independently would be sufficient, the pleading is not made insufficient by the insufficiency of one or more of the alternative statements.

As Restyled

If a party makes alternative statements, the pleading is sufficient if any one of them is sufficient.

Rule 71

When an order is made in favor of a person who is not a party to the action, that person may enforce obedience to the order by the same process as if a party; and, when obedience to an order may be lawfully enforced against a person who is not a party, that person is liable to the same process for enforcing obedience to the order as if a party.

As Restyled

When an order grants relief for a nonparty or may be enforced against a nonparty, the procedure for enforcing the order is the same as for a party.

The overarching style goals were to improve consistency and clarity and to draft the rules in a plainer, modern style. The Committee believes that those goals have been met, that the improvement is readily apparent, and that judges, lawyers, and law students will find the restyled rules much easier to use.

Formatting

Readers will immediately notice the difference in formatting. Look, for instance, at Rule 12(a) or 14(a). The restyled rules are better organized into subparts. They use more headings and subheadings to guide the reader. They use progressive left-side indents so that a rule's hierarchy is made graphic. They use more vertical lists. And the lists are always at the end of the sentence, never in midsentence as they are in current Rules 27(a)(1), 37(d), and 45(c)(3)(B).

Consistency

Consistency was a difficult challenge. Consistency is the cardinal rule of drafting, but after more than 70 years of amendments, the current rules have become stylistically inconsistent. To take a trivial example, the rules use *attorney fees*, *attorney's fees*, and *attorneys' fees*. Another example: the rules use *for cause shown*, *upon cause shown*, *for good cause*, and *for good cause shown*. Another example: the rules use *costs, including reasonable attorney's fees*; *reasonable costs and attorney's fees*; *reasonable expenses, including attorney's fees*; and *reasonable expenses, including a reasonable attorney's fee*. As a last example, the rules refer in various ways to the parties' *consent* or *agreement* or *stipulation*, sometimes with the qualifier *written* or *in writing* — for a total of six possibilities.

These examples could be multiplied almost endlessly. And in every instance, the Committee had to decide whether any difference was intended — or even what that difference might be. Often, it was fairly obvious that the inconsistency had no significance. When in doubt, the Committee asked one of its experts on procedure to research the question. If the Committee was then able to conclude that no difference was intended, the Committee used a single term. If the Committee could not be sure, it did not conform the terms, to avoid changing substantive meaning.

Rule 56 is an especially important example of the benefits of consistency. The standard set out in 56(c) is, of course, *no genuine issue as to any material fact*. But then 56(d) uses several variations on *no genuine issue*: *without substantial controversy, actually and in good faith controverted, not in controversy.* Restyled 56(d)(1) fixes the inconsistency by staying with *not genuinely at issue.*

To further achieve consistency, the restyled rules try to present parallel material in a parallel way. Current Rule 4(i)(2)(A) starts by addressing service on a United States agency, corporation, officer, or employee, but it changes the order of those four in the last part of the same sentence. Current Rule 33(b) addresses the content of an answer to an interrogatory, then the time for serving it; 34(b) reverses that order when addressing a response to a request for inspection. Current Rule 71A(c)(3) talks about furnishing at least one copy for the defendants' use; 71A(f) talks about furnishing for the defendants' use at least one copy. Some rules refer to a *hearing or trial*; others refer to a *trial or hearing.* The Committee could not possibly catch all the inconsistencies, but it hunted for them.

Intensifiers

Another difficult challenge was presented by what the Committee came to call "intensifiers." These are expressions that might seem to add emphasis but that, as a matter of good drafting, should be avoided for one of several reasons: they state the obvious, their import is so hard to grasp that it has no practical value, or they create negative implications for other rules. Examples (without citations):

- *the court may, in its discretion*: *May* means "has the discretion to"; *in its discretion* is a pure intensifier.
- *if the court deems it advisable, the court may*: Presumably, the court would not choose to do something inadvisable, so the *if*-clause is merely an intensifier.
- *the court may, in proper cases*: On the same theory, *in proper cases* is an intensifier.
- *unless the order expressly directs otherwise*: An order cannot implicitly direct; it means only what it says.

And using *expressly* suggests that this order is some-how different from all the other orders in the rules.

- *show affirmatively*: Likewise, this rule is not meant to be different from all the other rules that require a party or a document to merely *show*.

- *substantial justice*: *Substantial* seems to add nothing — or nothing appreciable.

- *reasonable written notice*: Using *reasonable* might imply that, in every other rule that requires notice, the notice does not have to be reasonable.

- *if, for any reason*: Here, too, *for any reason* adds nothing specific and might imply that the bare use of *if* in other rules means something else. Perhaps only some reasons are good in those other rules.

Again, the current rules contain many other examples. And again, the Committee considered each one individually to determine whether the intensifier had any practical significance.

Outdated and Repetitious Material

As you would expect, the Committee also tried to eliminate material that was outdated, redundant, or otherwise repetitious. Many of these decisions are reflected in the Committee Notes.

Some examples of outdated material or language in the current rules: the reference to *at law or in equity or in admiralty* in Rule 1; the reference to *demurrers, pleas, and exceptions* in Rule 7(c); the reference to *mesne process* in Rule 77(c); the limitation in Rule 80 to testimony that was *stenographically reported* (thus excluding other means of recording testimony); and the reference in Rule 81(f) to the now-abolished district director of internal revenue.

The current rules also contain a number of redundant — or self-evident — cross-references. Thus, Rule 7(b)(3) requires that motions "be signed in accordance with Rule 11."

But Rule 11 applies by its own terms to "every pleading, written motion, and other paper." Rule 8(b) states that a general denial is "subject to the obligations set forth in Rule 11." Of course it is; all pleadings are subject to Rule 11. Rule 33(b)(5) states that a party submitting interrogatories "may move for an order under Rule 37(a)." But Rule 37(a) allows sanctions for any failure to make disclosure or to cooperate in discovery. So why include the cross-reference to Rule 37 in just one or two discovery rules? The trouble with redundant cross-references is that there is no logical end to them.

The Committee tried to avoid or minimize repetition in various other ways as well:

- By shortening a second reference to the same thing. Thus, current Rule 72(a) allows a magistrate judge to issue an order and then refers three times to *the magistrate judge's order*. Since there's no other order involved, the restyled rule uses *the order* for the later references. The same principle applies to successive subparts: rather than seeming to start over with each one, we can generally trust the reader to read them together. Restyled Rule 4(d)(1) allows a plaintiff to *request that the defendant waive service of a summons*; in (d)(2), (3), and (4), we shorten to *the request* or *a waiver*. Restyled Rule 16(f)(1)(A) refers to *a scheduling or other pretrial conference*; in (B), we shorten to *the conference*.

- Similarly, by adopting shorter forms of reference. Rather than repeatedly referring to *the court from which the subpoena issued* in Rule 45, we use *the issuing court*. Rather than *the party who prevailed on that motion* in Rule 50(e), we use *the prevailing party*.

- By using a list that pulls repeated terms into the introduction to the list, where the term is used just once. Compare current and restyled Rule 45(a)(2).

- By merging two provisions that are essentially the same. Current Rules 26(g)(1) and (2) have three simi-

lar sentences about disclosure and discovery; the repetitious parts of those six sentences have been merged
into two sentences in restyled 26(g)(1). Likewise,
current Rules 37(a)(2)(A) and (B) have a similar sentence about certifying an effort to obtain disclosure or
discovery; those two sentences have been combined
into one in restyled 37(a)(1). Current Rule 50(b) uses
lists that repeat two items verbatim; the restyled rule
merges the repeated items into one list.

- By using more pronouns. After referring to *a copy of
the summons and of the complaint* in Rule 4(i)(1)(A)(i),
we use *a copy of each* in the subparts that immediately
follow. After referring to certain *materials* in Rule
26(b)(3)(A)(ii), we refer to obtaining *their substantial
equivalent* instead of *the substantial equivalent of the
materials.*

- By avoiding the purest form of repetition — saying
the same thing twice. Thus, current Rule 33(d) refers
to *an examination . . . or inspection.* The Committee
could see no appreciable difference between those
terms. The prime example may be current Rule 36,
which repeats in (a) and (b) that an admission is "for
purposes of the pending action only."

Once again, these examples could be multiplied.

Syntactic Ambiguity

The Committee tried to eliminate the syntactic ambiguities that lie hidden in the current rules. Some examples:

- Rule 11(c)(1)(B): *the court may enter an order describing the specific conduct that appears to violate subdivision (b) and directing an attorney, law firm, or party
to show cause why it has not violated subdivision (b)
with respect thereto.* What does *thereto* refer to?

- Rule 34(a): it's too long to quote, but the question is whether *in the possession, custody or control of the [responding] party* modifies *any designated documents.*

- Rule 45(c)(3)(B)(iii): is the material beginning with *the court may* supposed to modify all the items in the list or only item (iii)?

- Rule 46: *the action which the party desires the court to take or the party's objection to the action of the court and the grounds therefor.* What does *therefor* refer to?

- Rule 72(a): *any portion of the . . . order found to be clearly erroneous or contrary to law.* Does *clearly* modify *contrary to law?*

Other Kinds of Changes

Below is a short list of some of the other style principles that the Committee followed, trying to fix the more obvious deficiencies in the current rules:

- Reorganize jumbled provisions. For some examples, compare the current rules with restyled Rules 6(c), 8(b), 16(b), 23.1, 26(e), 30(b), 37(d), 44(a)(2), 45(c)(2)(B), and 70.

- Break up overlong sentences. Compare the current rules with restyled Rules 4(m), 6(b), 26(b)(3)(A), 26(b)(4)(B), 31(b), 34(a), 56(a), and 56(g). Of course, the added vertical lists in the restyled rules automatically break up their sentences into manageable pieces. No doubt some of the sentences are still too long, and even some of the vertical lists are more complicated than we might have liked (see Rule 4(f), for instance). But readers should notice a substantial overall improvement.

- Cut down on cross-references. The experts urge drafters to minimize cross-references, and the Committee tried to eliminate as many as it reasonably could. Current Rule 51, for instance, uses eight cross-references;

the restyled rule uses two. Again, a good many —
perhaps too many — cross-references still remain, but
many are gone.

- Minimize *of*-phrases. Garner's *Guidelines* puts it exactly like that. Thus, not *statute of the United States*,
but *federal statute*. Not *must include the names of all
the parties*, but *must name all the parties*. Not *after the
appearance of a defendant*, but *after any defendant
appears*. Not *the avoidance of unnecessary proof*, but
avoiding unnecessary proof. Not *order of the court*,
but *court order*.

- For the same reason, use possessives. The current
rules use possessives rather sparingly. The restyled
rules use them liberally. Not *the law of the foreign
country*, but *the foreign country's law*. Not *the pleadings of the defendants*, but *the defendants' pleadings*.
Not *the claims of the opposing party*, but *the opposing
party's claims*.

- Don't state the obvious. This is one more among the
many ways to omit unnecessary words. Current Rule
5(e): *The filing of papers* ~~with the court as required
by these rules~~ *shall be made by* (i.e., *A paper is filed
by*). Current Rule 6(b): *When* ~~by these rules or by a
notice given thereunder or by order of court~~ *an act is
required or allowed to be done* (i.e., *When an act may
or must be done*). Current Rule 26(b)(3) (after a sentence about a party's showing a need for materials): *In
ordering discovery of such materials* ~~when the required
showing has been made~~. Current Rule 30(b)(1): *shall
give . . . notice . . . to every other party* ~~to the action~~.
Current Rule 36(b): *Any admission* ~~made by a party~~
under this rule. Current Rule 56(a): *A party . . . may
. . . move . . . for a summary judgment* ~~in the party's
favor~~.

- Avoid legalese. No *pursuant to*. No *provided that*. No
such when it means "a" or "the." No *hereof* or *therefor*

or *wherein*. Consider this specimen, from current Rule 56(e): "Sworn or certified copies of all papers or parts thereof referred to in an affidavit shall be attached thereto or served therewith."

- Banish *shall*. The restyled civil rules, like the restyled appellate and criminal rules, use *must* instead of *shall*. *Shall* is notorious for its misuse and slipperiness in legal documents. No surprise, then, that the Committee changed *shall* to *may* in several instances, to *should* in several other instances, and to the simple present tense when the rule involves no obligation or permission (*There is one form of action; this order controls the course of the action*).

The Limits of Change

Renumbering

The Committee did not change any rule numbers, even though some of the rules (4, 23, 26, 71.1) are probably too long and others might benefit from repositioning. This also means that the Committee did not convert any of the interposed rules (4.1, 7.1, 23.1, 23.2, 44.1, and 65.1) to different numbers. Nor did it restore to active service the numbers of previously abrogated Rules 74, 75, and 76. At the rule level, the only change was from 71A to 71.1.

Any reordering was done at the subdivision level — (a), (b), (c) — or lower. Even then, the Committee changed only when it was satisfied that the improved sequencing outweighed the possible short-term inconvenience. Throughout this project, the Committee had to balance two competing interests. On the one hand, the current designations are familiar, and changing them will occasionally require users to make adjustments. On the other hand, this chance to set the rules in order — or better order — may not come along for another 70 years, and we should take the long view.

Consider just the first few changes. Current Rule 5(e) is merged into restyled 5(d) because both subdivisions deal with filing. Current Rules 6(d) and (e) move up because current 6(c) is empty. Current Rule 8(d) moves to restyled 8(b)(6) because it fits more logically with other materials on denials; and the change is ameliorated because the rule keeps its heading even at the paragraph level, (b)(6). The last sentences of current Rules 12(b) and (c) — two long sentences — are merged into restyled 12(d) because they are almost identical; and this change, too, is ameliorated by moving current 12(d) to a new 12(i). On the whole, the Committee tried to make a modest number of sensible changes in the subparts only.

Dealing with Uncertainty

As already suggested, the Committee had to repeatedly deal with ambiguities, inconsistencies, gaps, and other uncertainties in the current rules. Start with Rule 1 again — just two sentences. Should it be *These rules govern the procedure in all civil actions* or *in all civil actions and proceedings*? Should we change *inexpensive* to *economical*? Then Rule 2. One expert thought we should get rid of it entirely. Nothing in Rule 3. Rule 4(a). Would it be substantive to change *a failure to appear and defend* to *a failure to defend*? Is there a difference between *a failure to appear* and *failing to appear*? And so on.

Almost always, the Committee was able to answer these questions and clarify the rule or tighten the language. Occasionally, though, an ambiguity was so intractable that the Committee was not comfortable with changing the language. One memorable example: the two similar uses of *heretofore* in current Rule 59(a). The uses refer to the reasons for which new trials or rehearings *have heretofore been granted* in federal courts. This is classically bad drafting. Up until when? When the rule was first drafted? When the rule is applied? After research and extended discussion, the Committee

decided that it could not be sure, so that ambiguity — and
one piece of legalese — had to be carried forward.

Sacred Phrases

This was the Committee's name for phrases that have become so familiar as to be unalterably fixed in cement. They
are not exactly terms of art like *hearsay* and *bailment*. Terms
of art are typically confined to a given field, consist in one or
two words that are difficult to replace with one or two other
words, and convey a fairly precise and settled meaning. So-
called sacred phrases do not meet these criteria.

At any rate, some of the examples below could have easily been improved without changing the meaning; in others,
style improvements risked substantive change. But none
were touched.

- Restyled Rule 8(b)(5): *knowledge or information sufficient to form a belief.*
- Restyled Rule 12(b)(6): *failure to state a claim upon
  which relief can be granted.*
- Rule 13(a)(1)(A): *arises out of the transaction or occur-
  rence that is the subject matter of the opposing party's
  claim.*
- Restyled Rule 19(b): *in equity and good conscience.*
- Restyled Rule 44(b): *no record or entry of a specified
  tenor.*
- Restyled Rule 56(c): *there is no genuine issue as to any
  material fact.*

So that's how the Committee went about restyling the
civil rules. The Committee realizes that its work is not
done — but it trusts that readers will see the value of all that
has been done.

Lessons in Drafting from the New Federal Rules of Civil Procedure

This article was published in 2009. The examples in the text were accurate then, but the new rules (on the right side) could of course be amended as time goes on. That doesn't matter for the drafting lessons. The article had originally appeared as a five-part series in the Michigan Bar Journal. *The parts are marked with dingbats below, and each new part begins with a short introduction.*

December 1, 2007, was a historic day in the long, hard fight for better legal writing: the "restyled" Federal Rules of Civil Procedure — a top-to-bottom redraft — officially took effect. The project began in mid-2002 and was carried out by the Advisory Committee on Civil Rules. I was the drafting consultant, working with Joseph Spaniol. Bryan Garner had prepared an original draft in 1993, but the project was put on hold during restylings of the appellate and criminal rules.

Now, it's almost impossible to convey how excruciatingly careful our process was for redrafting the civil rules to improve their clarity, consistency, and readability — without making substantive changes. I outlined the process in a memo that accompanied the rules when they were published for comment in February 2005.[1] But even that outline doesn't capture the amount of work in my three 40- by 12-inch file drawers or the 775 documents in the final archive at the Administrative Office of the United States Courts.

What I can do is offer some drafting tips and examples from the new rules. My February 2005 memo touched on formatting, consistency, outdated and repetitious material,

---

[1] *See* the previous essay (using some examples that are naturally included in this later piece).

35

and (broadly) "other kinds of changes." In this article, I'll revisit everything, develop some old points, add some new ones, and try to provide a little advice. At the same time, I hope to put to rest any lingering doubts about whether this redrafting project was needed.

Just three caveats. First, nobody would claim that the new rules are perfect. You can always go back and find things that could be further improved. That said, the difference between the old and new rules is dramatic. (During the public-comment period, a class of students at WMU–Cooley Law School rated the clarity and readability of the old rules at 4.8 and the new rules at 8.4 on a scale of 1 to 10.) Second, if any mistakes were made in the restyling project, they can easily be fixed. Third, the examples below are just that — examples. They could be multiplied by many others from the old rules.

1. Put the parts in a logical order.

This may seem like an obvious principle, but the old rules violated it repeatedly — and right from the start. In the very first rule with any length — Rule 4 — there were three glaring examples.

First, old 4(a) put the last parts of a summons first. New 4(a) fixes that and uses a handy vertical list besides. (I'll get to vertical lists in the next guideline.)

Old 4(a)	New 4(a)(1)
(a) **Form.** The summons shall be signed by the clerk, bear the seal of the court, identify the court and the parties, be directed to the defendant, and state the name and address of the plaintiff's attorney or, if unrepresented, of the plaintiff. It shall also state the time within which the defendant must appear and defend, and notify the defendant that failure to do so will result in a judgment by default against the defendant for the relief demanded in the complaint. . . .	(a) **Contents; Amendments.** (1) *Contents.* A summons must: **(A)** name the court and the parties; **(B)** be directed to the defendant; **(C)** state the name and address of the plaintiff's attorney or — if unrepresented — of the plaintiff; **(D)** state the time within which the defendant must appear and defend; **(E)** notify the defendant that a failure to appear and defend will result in a default judgment against the defendant for the relief demanded in the complaint; **(F)** be signed by the clerk; and **(G)** bear the court's seal.

Second, old 4(d)(2) did the same thing: jumbled the requirements for a notice and request to waive service. The method of mailing, for instance, should come last, but it appeared second in a seven-item list. (I'll skip the example.)

Third, the paragraphs in old 4(d) followed this illogical progression:

- the effect of defendant's waiving service on an objection to venue or jurisdiction;
- how plaintiff requests a waiver;
- one consequence of defendant's failing to waive;
- the time for defendant to file an answer after returning a waiver;
- the results of plaintiff's filing the waiver (proof of service is not required); and
- a second consequence of defendant's failing to waive.

The order of the paragraphs in new 4(d):

- how plaintiff requests a waiver of service;
- the consequences of defendant's failing to waive;
- the time for defendant to file an answer after returning a waiver;
- the results of plaintiff's filing the waiver (proof of service is not required); and
- the effect of defendant's waiver on an objection to venue or jurisdiction.

This new order, by the way, is reflected in the headings to 4(d)(1)–(5). Old 4(d)(1)–(5) used no headings. If it had, the disorder might have been more apparent. In addition, separating the consequences of failing to waive produced repetition and unnecessary cross-references.

Old 4(d)(2) (last sentence) & (5)	New 4(d)(2)
(2) . . . If a defendant located within the United States fails to comply with a request for waiver made by a plaintiff located within the United States, the court shall impose the costs subsequently incurred in effecting service on the defendant unless good cause for the failure be shown. . . . (5) The costs to be imposed on a defendant under paragraph (2) for failure to comply with a request to waive service of a summons shall include the costs subsequently incurred in effecting service under subdivision (e), (f), or (h), together with the costs, including a reasonable attorney's fee, of any motion required to collect the costs of service.	(2) *Failure to Waive.* If a defendant located within the United States fails, without good cause, to sign and return a waiver requested by a plaintiff located within the United States, the court must impose on the defendant: **(A)** the expenses later incurred in making service; and **(B)** the reasonable expenses, including attorney's fees, of any motion required to collect those service expenses.

2. Use lists to the best advantage.

The vertical list is one of the drafter's — and reader's — best friends. Probably no other technique is more useful for organizing complex information, breaking it down into manageable chunks, avoiding repetition, and preventing ambiguity.

Take organization. Notice in this example how the exceptions are pulled together in the list and how the second sentence in the old rule is included within the third exception.

Old 6(d)	New 6(c)(1)
(d) For Motions — Affidavits. A written motion, other than one which may be heard ex parte, and notice of the hearing thereof shall be served not later than 5 days before the time specified for the hearing, unless a different period is fixed by these rules or by order of the court. Such an order may for cause shown be made on ex parte application. . . .	**(c) Motions, Notices of Hearing, and Affidavits.** (1) *In General.* A written motion and notice of the hearing must be served at least 5 days before the time specified for the hearing, with the following exceptions: **(A)** when the motion may be heard ex parte; **(B)** when these rules set a different time; or **(C)** when a court order — which a party may, for good cause, apply for ex parte — sets a different time.

In the next example, the list not only breaks up a ridiculously long sentence but also reorganizes the "failures" into two categories — failing to appear and failing to serve a paper.

Old 37(d)	New 37(d)(1)(A)

(d) **Failure of Party to Attend at Own Deposition or Serve Answers to Interrogatories or Respond to Request for Inspection.** If a party or an officer, director, or managing agent of a party or a person designated under Rule 30(b)(6) or 31(a) to testify on behalf of a party fails (1) to appear before the officer who is to take the deposition, after being served with a proper notice, or (2) to serve answers or objections to interrogatories submitted under Rule 33, after proper service of the interrogatories, or (3) to serve a written response to a request for inspection submitted under Rule 34, after proper service of the request, the court in which the action is pending on motion may make such orders in regard to the failure as are just, and among others it may take any action authorized under subparagraphs (A), (B), and (C) of subdivision (b)(2) of this rule. . . .	(d) **Party's Failure to Attend Its Own Deposition, Serve Answers to Interrogatories, or Respond to a Request for Inspection.**
	(1) *In General.*
	  (A) *Motion; Grounds for Sanctions.* The court where the action is pending may, on motion, order sanctions if:
	    (i) a party or a party's officer, director, or managing agent — or a person designated under Rule 30(b)(6) or 31(a)(4) — fails, after being served with proper notice, to appear for that person's deposition; or
	    (ii) a party, after being properly served with interrogatories under Rule 33 or a request for inspection under Rule 34, fails to serve its answers, objections, or written response.

Notice, too, that (1) in the new rule the subject of the independent clause (*the court*) is placed at the beginning rather than appearing midsentence and (2) the needless elaboration at the end of the old rule — 29 words beginning with *may make such orders* — is tightened to *may . . . order sanctions*.

Now consider the value of a list for avoiding repetition. Two examples follow. In the first example, the 89-word sentence in the old rule referred four times to a party or its attorney. (And the items were, again, not in a logical order.)

Old 16(f)	New 16(f)(1)
(f) Sanctions. *If a party or party's attorney* fails to obey a scheduling or pretrial order, or *if* no appearance is made *on behalf of a party* at a scheduling or pretrial conference, or *if a party or party's attorney* is substantially unprepared to participate in the conference, or *if a party or party's attorney* fails to participate in good faith, the judge, upon motion or the judge's own initiative, may make such orders with regard thereto as are just, and among others any of the orders provided in Rule 37(b)(2)(B), (C), (D). . . .	(f) **Sanctions.** (1) *In General.* On motion or on its own, the court may issue any just orders, including those authorized by Rule 37(b)(2)(A)(ii)–(vii), if a party or its attorney: (A) fails to appear at a scheduling or other pretrial conference; (B) is substantially unprepared to participate — or does not participate in good faith — in the conference; or (C) fails to obey a scheduling or other pretrial order.

Similarly, in the second example the old rule referred three times to determining capacity to sue or be sued.

Old 17(b)	New 17(b)
(b) Capacity to Sue or Be Sued. *The capacity* of an individual, other than one acting in a representative capacity, *to sue or be sued shall be determined* by the law of the individual's domicile. *The capacity* of a corporation *to sue or be sued shall be determined* by the law under which it was organized. In all other cases *capacity to sue or be sued shall be determined* by the law of the state in which the district court is held, except	**(b) Capacity to Sue or Be Sued.** Capacity to sue or be sued is determined as follows: (1) for an individual who is not acting in a representative capacity, by the law of the individual's domicile; (2) for a corporation, by the law under which it was organized; and (3) for all other parties, by the law of the state where the court is located, except . . . .

Next, an example of the value of a list for avoiding ambiguity. In the old rule, the words *which are in the possession, custody or control of the party* seemed to modify only *any designated tangible things* and not the earlier *any designated documents or electronically stored information.* The new rule gets the modification right with a list. (If only I could show you all the ambiguities in the old rules.)

Old 34(a)	New 34(a)
(a) Scope. Any party may serve on any other party a request (1) to produce and permit the party making the request, or someone acting on the requestor's behalf, to inspect, copy, test, or sample any designated documents or electronically stored information — including writings, drawings,	**(a) In General.** A party may serve on any other party a request within the scope of Rule 26(b): (1) to produce and permit the requesting party or its representative to inspect, copy, test, or sample *the following items in the re-*

graphs, charts, photographs, sound recordings, images, and other data or data compilations stored in any medium from which information can be obtained — translated, if necessary, by the respondent into reasonably usable form, or to inspect, copy, test, or sample any designated tangible things which constitute or contain matters within the scope of Rule 26(b) and *which are in the possession, custody or control of the party* upon whom the request is served; or (2) to permit entry upon designated land . . . .

sponding party's possession, custody, or control:

(A) any designated documents or electronically stored information — including writings, drawings, graphs, charts, photographs, sound recordings, images, and other data or data compilations — stored in any medium from which information can be obtained either directly or, if necessary, after translation by the responding party into a reasonably usable form; or

(B) any designated tangible things; or

(2) to permit entry onto designated land . . . .

Besides the ambiguity, the old rule repeated *inspect, copy, test, or sample*, and the word *translated* after the second dash connected in a clumsy, broken way with *information* before the first dash.

3. Break up long sentences.

This is standard advice for all forms of legal writing, since the ultralong sentence is one of our oldest and worst linguistic vices. My goal here is to look at some specific ways to cure it.

First way: simply convert a compound sentence using *and* into two sentences.

Old 27(b)	New 27(b)(3)
(b) **Pending Appeal.** . . . If the court finds that the perpetuation of the testimony is proper to avoid a failure or delay of justice, it may make an order allowing the depositions to be taken and may make orders of the character provided for by Rules 34 and 35, *and* thereupon the depositions may be taken and used in the same manner and under the same conditions as are prescribed in these rules for depositions taken in actions pending in the district court.	(3) *Court Order.* If the court finds that perpetuating the testimony may prevent a failure or delay of justice, the court may permit the depositions to be taken and may issue orders like those authorized by Rules 34 and 35. The depositions may be taken and used as any other deposition taken in a pending district-court action.

Second way: pull an exception into a new sentence, typically beginning with *But.*

Old 12(b)	New 12(b)
(b) **How Presented.** Every defense, in law or fact, to a claim for relief in any pleading, whether a claim, counterclaim, cross-claim, or third-party claim, shall be asserted in the responsive pleading thereto if one is required, except that the following defenses may at the option of the pleader be made by motion	(b) **How to Present Defenses.** Every defense to a claim for relief in any pleading must be asserted in the responsive pleading if one is required. *But* a party may assert the following defenses by motion . . . .

A variation on this second technique is to signal the main rule with a word like *Ordinarily* and put an exception or a condition in a second sentence beginning with *But*. The new rules may have innovated this technique; I have not seen it discussed in the literature.

Old 26(b)(3)	New 26(b)(3)(A)
(3) **Trial Preparation: Materials.** Subject to the provisions of subdivision (b)(4) of this rule, a party may obtain discovery of documents and tangible things otherwise discoverable under subdivision (b)(1) of this rule and prepared in anticipation of litigation or for trial by or for another party or by or for that other party's representative (including the other party's attorney, consultant, surety, indemnitor, insurer, or agent) only upon a showing that the party seeking discovery has substantial need of the materials in the preparation of the party's case and that the party is unable without undue hardship to obtain the substantial equivalent of the materials by other means. . . .	(3) *Trial Preparation: Materials.* **(A)** *Documents and Tangible Things.* Ordinarily, a party may not discover documents and tangible things that are prepared in anticipation of litigation or for trial by or for another party or its representative (including the other party's attorney, consultant, surety, indemnitor, insurer, or agent). *But,* subject to Rule 26(b)(4), those materials may be discovered if: (i) they are otherwise discoverable under Rule 26(b)(1); and (ii) the party shows that it has substantial need for the materials to prepare its case and cannot, without undue hardship, obtain their substantial equivalent by other means.

Third way, similar to the second one: pull a condition or conditions into a new sentence.

Old 12(f)	New 12(f)
(f) **Motion to Strike.** Upon motion made by a party before responding to a pleading or, if no responsive pleading is permitted by these rules, upon motion made by a party within 20 days after the service of the pleading upon the party or upon the court's own initiative at any time, the court may order stricken from any pleading any insufficient defense or any redundant, immaterial, impertinent, or scandalous matter.	(f) **Motion to Strike.** The court may strike from a pleading an insufficient defense or any redundant, immaterial, impertinent, or scandalous matter. The court may act: (1) on its own; or (2) on motion made by a party either before responding to the pleading or, if a response is not allowed, within 20 days after being served with the pleading.

Fourth way: repeat a key word from the previous sentence at or near the beginning of the new sentence.

Old 7(b)(1)	New 7(b)(1)
(b) **Motions and Other Papers.** (1) An application to the court for an order shall be by motion which, unless made during a hearing or trial, shall be made in writing, shall state with particularity the grounds therefor, and shall set forth the relief or order sought. . . .	(b) **Motions and Other Papers.** (1) *In General.* A request for a court order must be made by motion. *The motion* must: (A) be in writing unless made during a hearing or trial; (B) state with particularity the grounds for seeking the order; and (C) state the relief sought.

Finally, note that the vertical list, even when it does not serve any of the larger purposes described in guideline 2, still provides structure to a long sentence and makes the items easy to sort out and identify.

Old 5(c)	New 5(c)(1)
(c) Same: Numerous Defendants. In any action in which there are unusually large numbers of defendants, the court, upon motion or of its own initiative, may order that service of the pleadings of the defendants and replies thereto need not be made as between the defendants and that any cross-claim, counterclaim, or matter constituting an avoidance or affirmative defense contained *therein* shall be deemed to be denied or avoided by all other parties and that the filing of any such pleading and service thereof upon the plaintiff constitutes due notice of it to the parties. . . .	(c) Serving Numerous Defendants. (1) *In General.* If an action involves an unusually large number of defendants, the court may, on motion or on its own, order that: (A) defendants' pleadings and replies to them need not be served on other defendants; (B) any crossclaim, counterclaim, avoidance, or affirmative defense in those pleadings and replies to them will be treated as denied or avoided by all other parties; and (C) filing any such pleading and serving it on the plaintiff constitutes notice of the pleading to all parties.

As a last little challenge, can you quickly tell what the italicized *therein* referred to in the old rule? Ah, the false efficiency and pseudo-precision of legalese.

The old Federal Rules of Civil Procedure, which expired on December 1, 2007, are a gold mine — or should I say a landfill? — for examples of how not to draft. And it's inexcusable that generations of law students and young lawyers have had to wade through the clutter and confusion to learn civil procedure. The same goes for the Federal Rules of Evidence [before their restyling; *see* this book at 97], the Bankruptcy Code, most of the UCC, the Restatements, and just about all the rules, codes, and statutes that lawyers draft. Such a professional embarrassment. Such a waste of readers' time and effort.

Let's keep looking at ways to combat our affliction.

4. Avoid needless repetition.

Some of the repetition in the old civil rules is amazing. Below are four ways to deal with it. In each example, I'll italicize the repetition on the left.

Try a pronoun. (Incidentally, notice how the italicized items in the second sentence of the old rule weren't even in parallel order with the same items in the first sentence.)

Old 9(a)	New 9(a)
(a) **Capacity.** It is not necessary to aver the capacity of a party to sue or be sued or the authority of a party to sue or be sued in a representative capacity or the legal existence of an organized association of persons that is made a party, except to the extent required to show the jurisdiction of the court. *When a party desires to raise an issue as to the legal existence of any party or the capacity of any party to sue or*	(a) **Capacity or Authority to Sue; Legal Existence.** (1) *In General.* Except when required to show that the court has jurisdiction, a pleading need not allege: **(A)** a party's capacity to sue or be sued; **(B)** a party's authority to sue or be sued in a representative capacity; or

be sued or the authority of a party to sue or be sued in a representative capacity, the party desiring to raise the issue shall do so by	(C) the legal existence of an organized association of persons that is made a party. (2) **Raising Those Issues.** To raise any of *those* issues, a party must do so by . . . .

Similarly, try to shorten a second reference to the same thing. Old Rule 72(a), for instance, allowed a magistrate judge to issue an order and then referred three times to *the magistrate judge's order*; since there's no other order in sight, the new rule uses *the order* for the later references. Old Rule 23(e) used [*proposed*] *settlement, voluntary dismissal, or compromise* seven times; the new rule, after a first reference to *proposed settlement, voluntary dismissal, or compromise*, uses *the proposal.* Old Rule 45 referred six times to *the court from* [or *by*] *which the subpoena was issued*; the new rule, after a full first reference, uses *the issuing court*. New Rule 4(d)(1) allows the plaintiff to *request that the defendant waive service of a summons*; then in (d)(2), (3), and (4), that's shortened to *the request* or *a waiver*. These examples make an important point: rather than seeming to start over again with each successive subpart, as the old rules tended to do, we can generally trust the reader to read the subparts together as a coherent whole.

Another technique: try to merge two provisions that are essentially the same. The new rules do this many times.

Old 26(g)	New 26(g)
(g) Signing of Disclosures, Discovery Requests, Responses, and Objections. (1) Every disclosure made pursuant to subdivision (a)(1) or subdivision (a)(3) shall be signed by at least one attorney of record in the attorney's individual name, whose address shall be stated. An unrepresented party shall sign the disclosure and state the party's address. The signature of the attorney or party constitutes a certification that to the best of the signer's knowledge, information, and belief, formed after a reasonable inquiry, the disclosure is . . . . (2) Every discovery request, response, or objection *made by a party represented by an attorney shall be signed by at least one attorney of record in the attorney's individual name, whose address shall be stated. An unrepresented party shall sign the request, response, or objection and state the party's address. The signature of the attorney or party constitutes a certification that to the best of the signer's knowledge, information, and belief, formed after a reasonable inquiry, the request, response, or objection is . . . .*	**(g) Signing Disclosures and Discovery Requests, Responses, and Objections.** (1) *Signature Required; Effect of Signature.* Every disclosure under Rule 26(a)(1) or (a)(3) and every discovery request, response, or objection must be signed by at least one attorney of record in the attorney's own name — or by the party personally, if unrepresented — and must state the signer's address, e-mail address, and telephone number. By signing, an attorney or party certifies that to the best of the person's knowledge, information, and belief formed after a reasonable inquiry: **(A)** with respect to a disclosure, it is . . . ; and **(B)** with respect to a discovery request, response, or objection, it is . . . .

Old 37(a)(2)(A) & (B)	New 37(a)(1)
(a) **Motion For Order Compelling Disclosure or Discovery.** A party, upon reasonable notice to other parties and all persons affected thereby, may apply for an order compelling disclosure or discovery as follows: . . . **(2) Motion.** **(A)** If a party fails to make a disclosure required by Rule 26(a), any other party may move to compel disclosure and for appropriate sanctions. The motion must include a certification that the movant has in good faith conferred or attempted to confer with the party not making the disclosure in an effort to secure the disclosure without court action. **(B)** If a deponent fails to [make discovery in any of several ways], the discovering party may move for an order compelling an answer, or a designation, or an order compelling inspection in accordance with the request. *The motion must include a certification that the movant has in good faith conferred or attempted to confer with the person or party failing to make the discovery in an effort to secure the information or material without court action. . . .*	(a) **Motion for an Order Compelling Disclosure or Discovery.** (1) *In General.* On notice to other parties and all affected persons, a party may move for an order compelling disclosure or discovery. The motion must include a certification that the movant has in good faith conferred or attempted to confer with the person or party failing to make disclosure or discovery in an effort to obtain it without court action. [Subparagraphs 3(A) & (B) describe the two motions more specifically.]

Old 71	New 71
When an order is made in favor of a person who is not a party to the action, that person may enforce obedience to the order by the same process as if a party; *and, when obedience to an order* may be lawfully enforced against *a person who is not a party, that person is liable to the same process for enforcing obedience to the order as if a party.*	When an order grants relief for a nonparty or may be enforced against a nonparty, the procedure for enforcing the order is the same as for a party.

Finally, try a vertical list. As I illustrated in guideline 2, you can often pull repetitious language into the introduction to the list — and say it just once. Here's another example.

Old 30(g)	New 30(g)
(g) Failure to Attend or to Serve Subpoena; Expenses. (1) If the party giving the notice of the taking of a deposition fails to attend and proceed therewith and another party attends in person or by attorney pursuant to the notice, the court may order the party giving the notice to pay to such other party the reasonable expenses incurred by that party and that party's attorney in attending, including reasonable attorney's fees. *(2) If the party giving the notice of the taking of a deposition of a witness fails* to serve a subpoena upon the witness	**(g) Failure to Attend a Deposition or Serve a Subpoena; Expenses.** A party who, expecting a deposition to be taken, attends in person or by an attorney may recover reasonable expenses for attending, including attorney's fees, if the noticing party failed to: (1) attend and proceed with the deposition; or (2) serve a subpoena on a nonparty deponent, who consequently did not attend.

| and the witness because of such failure does not attend, *and if another party attends in person or by attorney because that party expects the deposition of that witness to be taken, the court may order the party giving the notice to pay to such other party the reasonable expenses incurred by that party and that party's attorney in attending, including reasonable attorney's fees.* | |

5. Don't state the obvious.

Lawyers are naturally careful in their drafting, trying to guard against the occasional reader in bad faith. But at some point, the misinterpretations become highly improbable, and the effort to prevent them is cumbersome and excessive. Some things are just too obvious for words.

Consider these examples from the old rules. I could go on and on.

- **5(e):** *The filing of papers* ~~with the court as required by these rules~~ *shall be made by* . . . (i.e., *A paper is filed by* . . .).
- **6(b):** *When* ~~by these rules or by a notice given thereunder or by order of court~~ *an act is required or allowed to be done at or within a specified time* . . . . (What are you trying to exclude? Why not simply *When an act may or must be done within a specified time?*)
- **7(b)(2):** *The rules applicable to captions and other matters of form of pleadings apply to all motions and other papers* ~~provided for by these rules.~~

- **7.1(a):** *A nongovernmental corporate party* ~~to an action or proceeding in a district court~~ *must file* . . . . (We know the world we're in — the district court.)

- **26(b)(3)** (after a sentence about a party's showing a need for materials): *In ordering discovery of such materials* ~~when the required showing has been made~~ . . . .

- **30(b)(1):** *shall give . . . notice . . . to every other party* ~~to the action~~.

- **36(b):** *Any admission* ~~made by a party~~ *under this rule* . . . .

- **38(d):** *A demand for trial by jury* ~~made as herein provided~~ *may not be withdrawn without the consent of the parties.*

- **41(d):** *the court may [order] the payment of costs . . . and may stay the proceedings* ~~in the action~~ *until the plaintiff has complied* ~~with the order~~.

- **46:** *Formal exceptions to rulings or orders* ~~of the court~~ *are unnecessary;* ~~but for all purposes for which an exception has heretofore been necessary~~ *it is sufficient that a party* . . . .

- **55(b)(2):** *the party . . . shall be served with written notice of the application for judgment at least 3 days prior to* [ugh] *the hearing* ~~on such~~ [ugh] ~~application~~.

- **56(a):** *A party . . . may . . . move . . . for a summary judgment* ~~in the party's favor~~ . . . .

The old rules also contained a number of self-evident — or redundant — cross-references. Thus, Rule 7(b)(3) required that motions "be signed in accordance with Rule 11." But Rule 11 applies by its own terms to "every pleading, written motion, and other paper." Rule 8(b) stated that a general denial is "subject to the obligations set forth in Rule 11." Of course it is; all pleadings are subject to Rule 11. Rule 33(b)(5) stated that a party submitting interrogatories "may move for an order under Rule 37(a)." But Rule 37(a) allows sanctions for any failure to make disclosure or to cooperate in discovery. So why include the cross-reference to Rule 37 in just one or two discovery rules? The trouble with redundant cross-references is that they may lead the reader to think they have special significance. Another trouble is that they tend to multiply.

6. Be clear; say what you mean in normal English.

Often in the old rules, you got the gist of the intended meaning, but you wondered why the drafter said it in such an odd or oblique way. What in the world impels lawyers to write like this?

- **4(l):** *If service is made by a person other than a United States marshal or deputy United States marshal, the person shall make affidavit thereof.*
- **7(a):** *There shall be a complaint . . . .*
- **8(c):** *In pleading to a preceding pleading . . . .*
- **18(b):** *Whenever a claim is one heretofore cognizable only after another claim has been prosecuted to a conclusion . . . .*
- **24(b):** *When a party to an action relies for ground of claim or defense upon any statute . . . .*
- **25(a)(1):** *Unless the motion for substitution is made not later than 90 days after the death is suggested upon the record by service of a statement of the fact of the death as provided herein for the service of the motion . . . .*
- **34(b):** *The response shall state, with respect to each item or category, that inspection and related activities will be permitted as requested, unless the request is objected to, including an objection to the requested form or forms for producing electronically stored information, stating the reasons for the objection.*

- **36(a):** *A denial shall fairly meet the substance of the requested admission . . . .*
- **38(b):** *Such demand may be indorsed upon a pleading of the party.*
- **52(a):** *due regard shall be given to the opportunity of the trial court to judge of the credibility of the witnesses.* (See if you can rewrite without using a single *of.*)

That goes to show why legal writing has been ridiculed for centuries — and why the new civil rules are cause for celebration.

At this point, let me digress momentarily and pose a question: why has most legal drafting been so bad for so long? The reasons number at least five.

First, law schools have traditionally neglected legal drafting. Even "neglected" is putting it rather mildly — "ignored" is more like it. Until the mid-1980s, most schools barely taught how to write memos and briefs. And until this century, few of them devoted any significant part of their writing programs to drafting (contracts, rules, and the like). Even now, only about half of schools do.[2]

Second, after law school most lawyers do not fill in the gap through self-education, by reading one of the good books on drafting, say, or even taking a CLE course. Rather, they tend to copy the old forms, thus continuing the cycle of

---

[2] *See* Ass'n of Legal Writing Directors & Legal Writing Inst., *Report of the Annual Legal Writing Survey* 13 (Question 20), 25 (Question 33) (2014), http://www.alwd.org (showing that 95 of 177 schools either give a drafting assignment or require a course in drafting).

bad drafting. Nobody should think that old forms must be tried and true — let alone well drafted.[3]

Third, young lawyers who learned the basics of plain English in law school may still have to "learn" drafting — or at least take direction — from older lawyers who never did learn those basics. The blind leading the partially sighted. (Again, I'm not talking about what substantive provisions to include, but how best to draft them.) In short, many or most lawyers still learn drafting on the job — a questionable practice:

> [S]tudents in the law schools should be taught how to draft legal documents, and should not be left to learn draftsmanship merely in the school of experience.
>
> Learning draftsmanship in the school of experience exclusively is costly to clients; it is costly to the public, and it is costly to the lawyer. It is like learning surgery by experience — it is possible, but it is tough on the patient, and tough on the reputation of the surgeon.[4]

Fourth, lawyers typically think they should draft for judges rather than the public or administrators or other front-end users. That, too, is a questionable strategy — and tends to produce poor drafting.[5]

Fifth, transactional lawyers seem to be less interested in skilled drafting than litigators are in writing skilled briefs or other court papers.[6] Maybe that's because litigators' briefs

---

[3] *See* Joseph Kimble, *The Great Myth That Plain Language Is Not Precise*, in *Lifting the Fog of Legalese: Essays on Plain Language* 37, 45 n.7 (2006) (citing authority for why forms are often unreliable and imprecise).

[4] Charles A. Beardsley, *Beware of, Eschew and Avoid Pompous Prolixity and Platitudinous Epistles!*, Cal. B.J., Mar. 1941, at 65, 65.

[5] *See* Bryan A. Garner, *Legal Writing in Plain English* 109 (2d ed. 2013) (describing five reasons why the strategy is "wrongheaded").

[6] *See* Bryan A. Garner, *President's Letter*, The Scrivener (newsletter of Scribes — Am. Soc'y of Legal Writers) 1, 1 (Winter 1998) (describing the author's CLE participants).

are regularly tested, so to speak, in court, while transactional documents rarely are. At any rate, the great disconnect is that while most transactional lawyers say that a very small percentage of the legal drafting they see is of a genuinely high quality, almost all of them would claim to produce high-quality documents.[7]

All in all, most lawyers — as smart, talented, and experienced as they may be — have a limited critical faculty when it comes to legal drafting. This article tries to raise awareness and offer some concrete help. Below are four more guidelines.

7. Keep the subject and verb — and the parts of the verb itself — close together.

It's standard advice to avoid creating wide gaps between the subject, verb, and object. Since these parts form the core of the sentence, the advice should be fairly obvious even to writers who aren't acquainted with the literature. But apparently not, judging from the old civil rules.

Interestingly, though, gaps between the subject and verb were much more common than gaps between the verb and object. So were gaps between the parts of the verb itself. (Note that a fairly short gap, a short insertion, may work fine: *the court may, for good cause, order that . . . .*)

Here, for example, are two mind-bending gaps between the main subject and verb.

---

[7] *Id.* at 3 (5% of the documents are of high quality; 95% would claim to produce high-quality documents).

Old 32(a)(2)	New 32(a)(3)
(2) The *deposition* of a party or of anyone who at the time of taking the deposition was an officer, director, or managing agent, or a person designated under Rule 30(b)(6) or 31(a) to testify on behalf of a public or private corporation, partnership or association or governmental agency which is a party *may be used* by an adverse party for any purpose.	(3) *Deposition of Party, Agent, or Designee.* An adverse *party may use* for any purpose the deposition of a party or anyone who, when deposed, was the party's officer, director, managing agent, or designee under Rule 30(b)(6) or 31(a)(4).

Notice how easy that fix was, using the active voice.

Old 44(b)	New 44(b)
(b) Lack of Record. A written *statement* that after diligent search no record or entry of a specified tenor is found to exist in the records designated by the statement, authenticated as provided in subdivision (a)(1) of this rule in the case of a domestic record, or complying with the requirements of subdivision (a)(2) of this rule for a summary in the case of a foreign record, *is* admissible as evidence that the records contain no such record or entry.	(b) Lack of a Record. A written *statement* that a diligent search of designated records revealed no record or entry of a specified tenor *is* admissible as evidence that the records contain no such record or entry. For domestic records, the statement must be authenticated under Rule 44(a)(1). For foreign records, the statement must comply with (a)(2)(C)(ii).

And here are two examples of big gaps between the parts of the main verb.

Old 16(b)	New 16(b)(1)
(b) Scheduling and Planning. Except in categories of actions exempted by district court rule as inappropriate, the district judge, or a magistrate judge when authorized by district court rule, *shall*, after receiving the report from the parties under Rule 26(f) or after consulting with the attorneys for the parties and any unrepresented parties by a scheduling conference, telephone, mail, or other suitable means, *enter* a scheduling order	**(b) Scheduling.** (1) *Scheduling Order.* Except in categories of actions exempted by local rule, the district judge — or a magistrate judge when authorized by local rule — *must issue* a scheduling order: (A) after receiving the parties' report under Rule 26(f); or (B) after consulting with the parties' attorneys and any unrepresented parties at a scheduling conference or by telephone, mail, or other means.

Old 56(a)	New 56(a)
(a) For Claimant. A party seeking to recover upon a claim, counterclaim, or cross-claim or to obtain a declaratory judgment *may*, at any time after the expiration of 20 days from the commencement of the action or after service of a motion for summary judgment by the adverse party, *move* with or without supporting affidavits for a summary judgment in the party's favor upon all or any part thereof.	**(a) By a Claiming Party.** A party claiming relief *may move*, with or without supporting affidavits, for summary judgment on all or part of the claim. The motion may be filed at any time after: (1) 20 days have passed from commencement of the action; or (2) the opposing party serves a motion for summary judgment.

New Rule 56(a) also illustrates two techniques, discussed in guideline 3, for breaking up long sentences: repeat or echo a key word from the previous sentence at the beginning of the new sentence (here *motion* echoes *move*); and pull conditions or qualifications into a new sentence.

8. Normally, don't put the main clause late in the sentence.

The main, or independent, clause is most typically delayed by piling up conditions or qualifiers at the beginning of the sentence. Again, guidelines 2 and 3 included some examples — old and new 37(d), 16(f), and 12(f). Here's one more (with the *if*s and the main subjects and verbs italicized).

Old 37(a)(2)(B)	New 37(a)(3)(B)
(B) *If* a deponent fails to answer a question propounded or submitted under Rules 30 or 31, or a corporation or other entity fails to make a designation under Rule 30(b)(6) or 31(a), or a party fails to answer an interrogatory submitted under Rule 33, *or if* a party, in response to a request for inspection submitted under Rule 34, fails to respond that inspection will be permitted as requested or fails to permit inspection as requested, the discovering *party may move* for an order compelling an answer, or a designation, or an order compelling inspection in accordance with the request. . . .	**(B)** *To Compel a Discovery Response.* A *party* seeking discovery *may move* for an order compelling an answer, designation, production, or inspection. This *motion may be made if*: **(i)** a deponent fails to answer a question asked under Rule 30 or 31; **(ii)** a corporation or other entity fails to make a designation under Rule 30(b)(6) or 31(a)(4); **(iii)** a party fails to answer an interrogatory submitted under Rule 33; or **(iv)** a party fails to respond that inspection will be permitted — or fails to permit inspection — as requested under Rule 34.

If the condition or conditions are reasonably short (as in this sentence), then putting them at the beginning of the sentence will not tax the reader's memory. But a long condition belongs at the end, after the main clause.

Old 55(b)(2)	New 55(b)(2)
(2) **By the Court.** . . . *If*, in order to enable the court to enter judgment or to carry it into effect, it is necessary to take an account or to determine the amount of damages or to establish the truth of any averment by evidence or to make an investigation of any other matter, the *court may conduct* such hearings or order such references as it deems necessary and proper	(2) *By the Court.* . . . The *court may conduct* hearings or make referrals . . . *when*, to enter or effectuate judgment, it needs to: (A) conduct an accounting; (B) determine the amount of damages; (C) establish the truth of any allegation by evidence; or (D) investigate any other matter.

9. Try to put statements in positive form.

Avoid multiple negatives — that's another standard guideline that the old rules often ignored. Below are several common patterns for multiple negatives. Remember that besides *no*, *not*, and words with negative prefixes (*in-*, *un-*, *non-*), words like *unless*, *without*, *absent*, *fail*, and *preclude* also have negative force.

Pattern 1: *shall/may not . . . unless/without/if . . . not.*

Old 38(d)	New 38(d)
(d) **Waiver.** The failure of a party to serve and file a demand as required by this rule constitutes a waiver by the party of trial by jury. A demand for trial by jury made as herein provided *may not* be withdrawn *without* the consent of the parties.	(d) **Waiver; Withdrawal.** A party waives a jury trial unless its demand is properly served and filed. A proper demand may be withdrawn only if the parties consent.

The next example — if you can believe it — used *save* in its archaic negative sense.

Old 41(a)(2)	New 41(a)(2)
(2) **By Order of Court.** Except as provided in paragraph (1) of this subdivision of this rule, an action *shall not* be dismissed at the plaintiff's instance *save* upon order of the court and upon such terms and conditions as the court deems proper. . . .	(2) *By Court Order; Effect.* Except as provided in Rule 41(a)(1), an action may be dismissed at the plaintiff's request only by court order, on terms that the court considers proper. . . .

Pattern 2: *no* _____ *shall/may . . . unless/without/if . . . not.*

Old 55(b)(2)	New 55(b)(2)
(2) By the Court. In all other cases the party entitled to a judgment by default shall apply to the court therefor; but *no* judgment by default *shall* be entered against an infant or incompetent person *unless* represented in the action by a general guardian, committee, conservator, or other such representative who has appeared therein. . . .	**(2) *By the Court.*** In all other cases, the party must apply to the court for a default judgment. A default judgment may be entered against a minor or incompetent person only if represented by a general guardian, conservator, or other like fiduciary who has appeared. . . .

Pattern 3: *no* _____ */nothing . . . prevents/precludes.*

Old 50(d)	New 50(e)
(d) Same: Denial of Motion for Judgment as a Matter of Law. . . . If the appellate court reverses the judgment, *nothing* in this rule *precludes* it from determining that the appellee is entitled to a new trial	**(e) Denying the Motion for Judgment as a Matter of Law; Reversal on Appeal.** . . . If the appellate court reverses the judgment, it may order a new trial . . . .

Pattern 4: *unless . . . is not.*

Old 11(c)(1)(A)	New 11(c)(2)
(A) By Motion. A motion for sanctions . . . shall be served as provided in Rule 5, but shall *not* be filed with or presented to the court *unless,* within 21 days after service of the motion (or such other period as the court may prescribe), the challenged paper, claim, defense, contention, allegation, or denial *is not* withdrawn or appropriately corrected. . . .	**(2) *Motion for Sanctions.*** A motion for sanctions . . . must be served under Rule 5, but it must not be filed or be presented to the court if the challenged paper, claim, defense, contention, or denial is withdrawn or appropriately corrected within 21 days after service or within another time the court sets. . . .

You may have noticed that the last example actually used three negatives. That's right — the rare triple negative. For your reading pleasure, behold one more.

Old 8(e)(2)	New 8(d)(2)
(2) . . . When two or more statements are made in the alternative and one of them if made independently would be sufficient, the pleading is *not* made *insufficient* by the *insufficiency* of one or more of the alternative statements. . . .	**(2) *Alternative Statements of a Claim or Defense.*** . . . If a party makes alternative statements, the pleading is sufficient if any one of them is sufficient.

10. Minimize cross-references.

Most readers will tell you, if you care to ask, that unnecessary cross-references are at least distracting and at worst irritating. They distract by cluttering the sentence and directing the reader's attention elsewhere. And they irritate when the reader realizes that the reference was to something already known or entirely obvious.

The prime reason for unnecessary cross-references is an unwillingness to trust the reader to read successive subparts together, as if each textual sliver had to stand alone in the world. Thus, you get drafting like this.

Old 53(h)(1) & (2)	New 53(g)(1) & (2)

(h) Compensation.
 	
    (1) Fixing Compensation. The court must fix the master's compensation before or after judgment on the basis and terms stated in the order of appointment . . . .
 	
    (2) Payment. The compensation fixed under Rule 53(h)(1) must be paid . . . .
	(g) Compensation.
	
	    (1) *Fixing Compensation.* Before or after judgment, the court must fix the master's compensation on the basis and terms stated in the appointing order . . . .
	
	    (2) *Payment.* The compensation must be paid . . . .

Old 51(c)(2) & (d)	New 51(c)(2) & (d)

(2) An objection is timely if:
 	
    (A) a party that has been informed of an instruction or action on a request before the jury is instructed and before final jury arguments, as provided by Rule 51(b)(1), objects at the opportunity for objection required by Rule 51(b)(2); or
 	
    (B) a party that has not been informed of an instruction or action on a request before the time for objection provided by Rule 51(b)(2)
	(2) *When to Make.* An objection is timely if:
	
	    (A) a party objects at the opportunity provided under Rule 51(b)(2); or
	
	    (B) a party was not informed of an instruction or action on a request before that opportunity to object, and the party objects promptly after learning that the instruction or request will be, or has been, given or refused.

objects promptly after learning that the instruction or request will be, or has been, given or refused.

(d) Assigning Error; Plain Error.

(1) A party may assign as error:

(A) an error in an instruction actually given if that party made a proper objection under Rule 51(c), or

(B) a failure to give an instruction if that party made a proper request under Rule 51(a), and — unless the court made a definitive ruling on the record rejecting the request — also made a proper objection under Rule 51(c).

(d) Assigning Error; Plain Error.

(1) *Assigning Error.* A party may assign as error:

(A) an error in an instruction actually given, if that party properly objected; or

(B) a failure to give an instruction, if that party properly requested it and — unless the court rejected the request in a definitive ruling on the record — also properly objected.

The new rules may still have too many cross-references, but they have about 45 fewer than the old rules. That's progress.

The advice in this next part, guidelines 11 through 13, will be all about omitting needless words — about tightening. And here the examples below can't begin to do justice to the restyling project, because just about every other sentence seemed to have extra words. So it's a real challenge to choose from all the possible examples.

Consider this: the old rules had about 45,500 words; the new rules, even with the much greater use of headings, have about 39,280. That's 6,220 fewer words, or almost 14% less — all while following the Advisory Committee's mandate to not change substantive meaning.

Of course, writing clearly and plainly does not necessarily mean always using the fewest possible words in every sentence. But it would be surprising to learn of a plain-language project that did not produce a significant reduction overall.

Finally, remember that two of the guidelines discussed earlier — avoid needless repetition (#4) and don't state the obvious (#5) — also bear on omitting needless words.

11. Root out unnecessary prepositional phrases. Question every *of*.

There's no surer way to tighten legal writing than to eliminate unnecessary prepositional phrases. And as simple as it may sound, there's no better indicator than the word *of*.

Old 4(d)(1)	New 4(d)(5)
(1) A defendant who waives service *of* a summons does not thereby waive any objection *to* the venue or *to* the jurisdiction *of* the court *over* the person *of* the defendant.	(5) *Jurisdiction and Venue Not Waived.* Waiving service *of* a summons does not waive any objection *to* personal jurisdiction or *to* venue.

Old 10(a)	New 10(a)
(a) Caption; Names of Parties. . . . *In* the complaint the title *of* the action shall include the names *of* all the parties, but *in* other pleadings it is sufficient *to* state the name *of* the first party *on* each side *with* an appropriate indication *of* other parties.	**(a) Caption; Names of Parties.** . . . The title *of* the complaint must name all the parties; the title *of* other pleadings, after naming the first party *on* each side, may refer generally *to* other parties.

Old 16(b)(8)	New 16(b)(3)(B)(vi)
. . . The scheduling order . . . may include . . . any other matters appropriate *in* the circumstances *of* the case.	The scheduling order may . . . include other appropriate matters.

Old 35(b)(3)	New 35(b)(6)
(3) . . . This subdivision does not preclude discovery *of* a report *of* an examiner or the taking *of* a deposition *of* the examiner *in accordance with* the provisions *of* any other rule.	**(6)** . . . This subdivision does not preclude obtaining an examiner's report or deposing an examiner *under* other rules.

Old 45(b)(1)	New 45(b)(1)
(1) A subpoena may be served *by* any person who is not a party and is not less than 18 years *of* age. Service *of* a subpoena *upon* a person named therein shall be made *by* delivering a copy thereof *to* such person	**(1)** *By Whom; Tendering Fees; Serving a Copy of Certain Subpoenas.* Any person who is at least 18 years old and not a party may serve a subpoena. Serving a subpoena requires delivering a copy *to* the named person . . . .

Old 54(d)(2)(C)	New 54(d)(2)(C)
(C)... The court may determine issues *of* liability *for* fees *before* receiving submissions bearing *on* issues *of* evaluation *of* services *for* which liability is imposed *by* the court....	(C)*Proceedings.* ... The court may decide issues *of* liability *for* fees *before* receiving submissions *on* the value *of* services....

One good, recurring way to minimize *of*-phrases is to use possessives. The new rules convert dozens and dozens of *of*-phrases — and other prepositional phrases — to possessives. Some examples:

- **4(f)(2)(A):** *the law of the foreign country/the foreign country's law.*

- **5(c); now 5(c)(1)(A):** *the pleadings of the defendants/ defendants' pleadings.*

- **13(i):** *the claims of the opposing party/the opposing party's claims.*

- **24(b); now 24(b)(3):** *the rights of the original parties/ the original parties' rights.*

- **26(a)(2)(B); now 26(a)(2)(B)(iv):** *the qualifications of the witness/the witness's qualifications.*

- **26(b)(3); now 26(b)(3)(C):** *a statement . . . previously made by that person/the person's own previous statement.*

- **28(c):** *a relative or employee or attorney or counsel of any of the parties/any party's relative, employee, or attorney.*

- **35(b)(2):** *a report of the examination so ordered/the examiner's report.*

- **60(a):** *with leave of the appellate court/with the appellate court's leave.*

A second — and similar — technique for minimizing *of*-phrases and other prepositional phrases: convert them to adjectives. Of course, some of the phrases are used repeatedly.

- **4(d)(1); now 4(d)(5):** *the jurisdiction of the court over the person of the defendant/personal jurisdiction.*
- **4(k)(1)(D); now 4(k)(1)(C):** *a statute of the United States/a federal statute.*
- **26(b); now 26(b)(1):** *by order of the court/by court order.*
- **32(a)(4); now 32(a)(8):** *action . . . in any court of the United States or of any State/any federal- or state-court action.*
- **38(b):** *trial by jury/jury trial.*
- **54(c):** *judgment by default/default judgment.*
- **57:** *an action for a declaratory judgment/a declaratory-judgment action.*
- **63:** *trial without a jury/nonjury trial.*
- **69(a); now 69(a)(1):** *a judgment for the payment of money/a money judgment.*

A third technique: convert [article] [noun] *of* into an *-ing* form.

- **11(c)(2)(A); now 11(c)(5)(A):** *for a violation of subdivision (b)(2)/for violating Rule 11(b)(2).*
- **16(c)(4); now 16(c)(2)(D):** *the avoidance of unnecessary proof/avoiding unnecessary proof.*
- **16(c)(7); now 16(c)(2)(G):** *the identification of witnesses/identifying witnesses.*
- **23.2:** *in the conduct of the action/in conducting the action.*
- **37(g); now 37(f):** *the development and submission of a proposed discovery plan/developing and submitting a proposed discovery plan.*
- **61:** *no error in either the admission or the exclusion of evidence/no error in admitting or excluding evidence.*

12. Replace multiword prepositions.

Multiword prepositions — also called compound or complex or phrasal prepositions — are pervasive in legal writing.[8] One writer calls them the "compost of our language."[9] You can almost always replace them with a simpler preposition, the one that you would probably use in speech.

- 4(i)(3); now 4(i)(4): *for the purpose of curing the failure/to cure its failure.*

- 16(c); now 16(c)(2): *take appropriate action with respect to/take appropriate action on.*

- 16(c), last sentence; now 16(c)(1): *in order to consider possible settlement/to consider possible settlement.*

- 16(c)(13); now 16(c)(2)(M): *a separate trial pursuant to Rule 42(b)/a separate trial under Rule 42(b).* [Imagine how many times this one occurs.]

- 26(a)(1), last paragraph; now 26(a)(1)(C): *in the circumstances of the action/in this action.*

- 26(a)(3)(B); now 26(a)(3)(A)(ii): *whose testimony is expected to be presented by means of a deposition/whose testimony the party expects to present by deposition.*

- 30(c); now 30(c)(1): *under the provisions of the Federal Rules of Evidence/under the Federal Rules of Evidence.*

- 32(a)(3)(E); now 32(a)(4)(E): *such exceptional circumstances exist as to make it desirable/exceptional circumstances make it desirable.*

- 35(b)(3); now 35(b)(6): *in accordance with the provisions of any other rule/under other rules.*

- 41(a)(2): *prior to the service upon the defendant of the plaintiff's motion to dismiss/before being served with the plaintiff's motion to dismiss.*

---

[8] For a long list, see Kimble, *Plain Words*, in *Lifting the Fog of Legalese* at 170–71.

[9] C. Edward Good, *Mightier Than the Sword* 73 (1989).

- **44(b):** *in the case of* a domestic record/*for* domestic records.

- **64; now 64(a):** *during the course of* an action/*throughout* an action.

- **71:** *in favor of* a person who is not a party to the action/ *for* a nonparty.

13. Collapse clauses into a word or two when possible.

Here are a handful of examples:

- **11(c)(3); now 11(c)(6):** *the conduct determined to constitute a violation of this rule/the sanctioned conduct.*

- **11(d):** *motions that are subject to the provisions of Rules 26 through 37/motions under Rules 26 through 37.*

- **14(a); now 14(a)(1):** *a person not a party to the action/ a nonparty.*

- **26(a)(1)(D); now 26(a)(1)(A)(iv):** *a judgment which may be entered/a possible judgment.*

- **26(g)(3):** *the person who made the certification/the signer.*

- **30(a)(2); now 30(a)(2)(B):** *the person to be examined/ the deponent.*

- **33(b)(3); now 33(b)(2):** *the party upon whom the interrogatories have been served/the responding party.*

- **45(b)(3); now 45(b)(4):** *the court by which the subpoena is issued/the issuing court.*

- **50(d); now 50(e):** *the party who prevailed on that motion/the prevailing party.*

Let's return to our general prescription to omit needless words. By combining all the techniques for doing that — and trying to say what you mean simply and directly — we produce differences like this.

Old 12(a)(2)	New 12(a)(1)(B)
(2) A party served with a pleading stating a cross-claim against that party shall serve an answer thereto within 20 days after being served. The plaintiff shall serve a reply to a counterclaim in the answer within 20 days after service of the answer . . . . [43 words]	(B) A party must serve an answer to a counterclaim or crossclaim within 20 days after being served with the pleading that states the counterclaim or crossclaim. [26 words]

Old 25(a)(2)	New 25(a)(2)
(2) In the event of the death of one or more of the plaintiffs or of one or more of the defendants in an action in which the right sought to be enforced survives only to the surviving plaintiffs or only against the surviving defendants, the action does not abate. . . . [49 words]	(2) *Continuation Among the Remaining Parties.* After a party's death, if the right sought to be enforced survives only to or against the remaining parties, the action does not abate . . . . [24 words]

Old 35(b)(2)	New 35(b)(4)
(2) By requesting and obtaining a report of the examination so ordered or by taking the deposition of the examiner, the party examined waives any privilege the party may have in that action or any other involving the same controversy, regarding the testimony of every other person who has examined or may thereafter examine the party in respect of the same mental or physical condition. [64 words]	(4) *Waiver of Privilege.* By requesting and obtaining the examiner's report, or by deposing the examiner, the party examined waives any privilege it may have — in that action or any other action involving the same controversy — concerning testimony about all examinations of the same condition. [41 words]

Old 39(a)	New 39(a)
(a) **By Jury.** When trial by jury has been demanded as provided in Rule 38, the action shall be designated upon the docket as a jury action. The trial of all issues so demanded shall be by jury, unless (1) the parties or their attorneys of record, by written stipulation filed with the court or by an oral stipulation made in open court and entered in the record, consent to trial by the court sitting without a jury or (2) the court upon motion or of its own initiative finds that a right of trial by jury of some or all of those issues does not exist under the Constitution or statutes of the United States. [111 words]	(a) **When a Demand Is Made.** When a jury trial has been demanded under Rule 38, the action must be designated on the docket as a jury action. The trial on all issues so demanded must be by jury unless: (1) the parties or their attorneys file a stipulation to a nonjury trial or so stipulate on the record; or (2) the court, on motion or on its own, finds that on some or all of those issues there is no federal right to a jury trial. [79 words]

Old 62(f)	New 62(f)
(f) **Stay According to State Law.** In any state in which a judgment is a lien upon the property of the judgment debtor and in which the judgment debtor is entitled to a stay of execution, a judgment debtor is entitled, in the district court held therein, to such stay as would be accorded the judgment debtor had the action been maintained in the courts of that state. [62 words]	(f) **Stay in Favor of a Judgment Debtor Under State Law.** If a judgment is a lien on the judgment debtor's property under the law of the state where the court is located, the judgment debtor is entitled to the same stay of execution the state court would give. [38 words]

Old 64	New 64(a)
At the commencement of and during the course of an action, all remedies providing for seizure of person or property for the purpose of securing satisfaction of the judgment ultimately to be entered in the action are available under the circumstances and in the manner provided by the law of the state in which the district court is held, existing at the time the remedy is sought . . . . [67 words]	(a) **Remedies Under State Law — In General.** At the commencement of and throughout an action, every remedy is available that, under the law of the state where the court is located, provides for seizing a person or property to secure satisfaction of the potential judgment. . . . [38 words]

Old 65(a)(2)	New 65(a)(2)
(2) **Consolidation of Hearing With Trial on Merits.** . . . This subdivision (a)(2) shall be so construed and applied as to save to the parties any rights they may have to trial by jury. [23 words]	(2) *Consolidating the Hearing with the Trial on the Merits.* . . . But the court must preserve any party's right to a jury trial. [12 words]

Old 71A(k)	New 71.1(k)
(k) Condemnation Under a State's Power of Eminent Domain. The practice as herein prescribed governs in actions involving the exercise of the power of eminent domain under the law of a state, provided that if the state law makes provision for trial of any issue by jury, or for trial of the issue of compensation by jury or commission or both, that provision shall be followed. [57 words]	**(k) Condemnation Under a State's Power of Eminent Domain.** This rule governs an action involving eminent domain under state law. But if state law provides for trying an issue by jury — or for trying the issue of compensation by jury or commission or both — that law governs. [38 words]

How about that? Imagine the effect on generations of law students who, for three years, have had to labor through drafting bogs like those on the left, thinking they must be perfectly good and normal.

I'll end my drafting lessons with this fifth part. But there is still so much — so many improvements on the old civil rules — that I haven't been able to cover. I haven't, for instance, covered the rampant inconsistencies in the old rules. Among them:

- *for cause shown; upon cause shown; for good cause; for good cause shown.*
- *on motion; on application.*
- *court orders; court directs.*
- *make orders; issue orders.*
- *counsel; attorney.*
- *costs, including reasonable attorney's fees; reasonable costs and attorney's fees; reasonable expenses, includ-*

ing attorney's fees; reasonable expenses, including a reasonable attorney's fee.

- *no genuine issue as to any material fact; without substantial controversy; actually and in good faith controverted; not in controversy.*

Nor have I been able to catalogue the many syntactic ambiguities in the old rules. I offered several examples in my February 2005 *Guiding Principles* memo,[10] and there's one at the end of guideline 2 earlier, but those are only a start.

Some of the improvements in the new rules — especially the structural changes — can't be easily illustrated. But if you'd like to see the striking difference made by reorganizing jumbled provisions, compare the old rules with new 6(c), 8(b), 16(b), 23.1, 26(e), 30(b), 37(d), 44(a)(2), 45(c)(2)(B), 52(a), and 70. More specifically, let me offer just one example of the greater coherence that comes from grouping related items — here, general or routine authority (versus sanctioning authority).

Old 53(c) & (d)	New 53(c)
(c) **Master's Authority.** Unless the appointing order expressly directs otherwise, a master has authority to regulate all proceedings and take all appropriate measures to perform fairly and efficiently the assigned duties. The master may by order impose upon a party any noncontempt sanction provided by Rule 37 or 45, and may recommend a contempt sanction against a party and sanctions against a nonparty.	(c) Master's Authority. (1) *In General.* Unless the appointing order directs otherwise, a master may: (A) regulate all proceedings; (B) take all appropriate measures to perform the assigned duties fairly and efficiently; and (C) if conducting an evidentiary hearing, exercise the appointing

---

10   *See* this book at 29–30.

(d) Evidentiary Hearings. Unless the appointing order expressly directs otherwise, a master conducting an evidentiary hearing may exercise the power of the appointing court to compel, take, and record evidence.

court's power to compel, take, and record evidence.

(2) *Sanctions.* The master may by order impose on a party any noncontempt sanction provided by Rule 37 or 45, and may recommend a contempt sanction against a party and sanctions against a nonparty.

For more of the same, compare the old rules with new 30(c) & (d) (grouping the materials on objections in (c) only); new 37(b)(2)(A) & (B) (breaking out the illogical grouping in old (b)(2)(C) & (E)); new 37(c)(1) (grouping the sanctions into a list); and new 52(a) (grouping the last sentence of old (b) with the other material on findings and conclusions). The organizational changes — even without changing any of the main numbers — have significantly transformed the rules.

Finally, this article has barely touched on formatting. I'll do that in guideline 14 below, but the new rules are designed to make it much easier to see how everything fits together. They are broken down into more levels — hence the greater use of headings and subheadings; they use progressive, or cascading, indents to show subparts and sub-subparts; they use hanging indents so that all the lines in a subpart or a list are indented the same as the first word in the first line (see new 53(c) above); they use many more vertical lists; and the lists are always at the end of the sentence, never in the middle.

Unfortunately, in most of the academic pamphlets containing the new rules, the publishers have largely mangled the intended formatting. That's quite a disappointment after the concerted effort we made.

In any event, here are six more guidelines.

14. Use informative headings and subheadings.

Good headings and subheadings are vital navigational aids for the reader. The old rules had 359 of them; the new rules have 757. Just to illustrate their value:

Old 8(b)	New 8(b)
(b) Defenses; Form of Denials.	(b) Defenses; Admissions and Denials. (1) *In General.* (2) *Denials — Responding to the Substance.* (3) *General and Specific Denials.* (4) *Denying Part of an Allegation.* (5) *Lacking Knowledge or Information.* (6) *Effect of Failing to Deny.*

Old 16(b)	New 16(b)
(b) Scheduling and Planning.	(b) Scheduling. (1) *Scheduling Order.* (2) *Time to Issue.* (3) *Contents of the Order.* (A) *Required Contents.* (B) *Permitted Contents.* (4) *Modifying a Schedule.*

Old 26(a)	New 26(a)
(a) Required Disclosures; Methods to Discover Additional Matter. (1) Initial Disclosures. (2) Disclosure of Expert Testimony. (3) Pretrial Disclosures. (4) Form of Disclosures. (5) [Now deleted]	(a) Required Disclosures. (1) *Initial Disclosure.* (A) *In General.* (B) *Proceedings Exempt from Initial Disclosure.* (C) *Time for Initial Disclosures — In General.* (D) *Time for Initial Disclosures — For Parties Served or Joined Later.* (E) *Basis for Initial Disclosure; Unacceptable Excuses.* (2) *Disclosure of Expert Testimony.* (A) *In General.* (B) *Written Report.* (C) *Time to Disclose Expert Testimony.* (D) *Supplementing the Disclosure.* (3) *Pretrial Disclosures.* (A) *In General.* (B) *Time for Pretrial Disclosures; Objections.* (4) *Form of Disclosures.*

Old 31(a)	New 31(a)
(a) Serving Questions; Notice.	(a) **When a Deposition May Be Taken.** (1) *Without Leave.* (2) *With Leave.* (3) *Service; Required Notice.* (4) *Questions Directed to an Organization.* (5) *Questions from Other Parties.*

Old 68 [about offer of judgment]	New 68
	(a) Making an Offer; Judgment on an Accepted Offer. (b) Unaccepted Offer. (c) Offer After Liability Is Determined. (d) Paying Costs After an Unaccepted Offer.

15. Be wary of intensifiers.

Intensifiers are expressions that may seem to add emphasis but that, as a matter of good drafting, should be minimized for any of several reasons: they state the obvious, their import is so hard to grasp that it has no practical value, or they create negative implications for other rules.

- **4(d)(2)(A):** *The notice . . . shall be in writing and shall be addressed <u>directly</u> to the defendant.* How would you address a written notice indirectly?

- **6(a)**: *any period of time prescribed . . . by any <u>applicable</u> statute.* Are we concerned about an inapplicable statute?

- **6(b)** (and several other rules): *the court . . . may . . . <u>in its discretion</u>. May* means "has the discretion to"; *in its discretion* is a pure intensifier.

- **12(b)**: *may <u>at the option of the pleader</u>.* Same theory.

- **15(d)**: <u>*If the court deems it advisable . . .* </u> *, it shall so order.* Presumably, the court would not choose to do something inadvisable.

- **41(d)**: *the court may make such order for the payment of costs . . . <u>as it may deem proper</u>.* Same theory.

- **53(c) & (d)**: *Unless the appointing order <u>expressly</u> directs otherwise.* An order cannot implicitly direct; it means only what it says. And using *expressly* suggests that this order is somehow different from all the other orders in the rules.

- **56(e)**: *affidavits . . . shall show <u>affirmatively</u>.* Likewise, this rule is not meant to be different from all the other rules that require a party or a document to merely show.

- **61**: *inconsistent with <u>substantial</u> justice. Substantial* seems to add nothing — or nothing appreciable.

- **70**: *The court may . . . <u>in proper cases</u>.* The same theory as in 15(d) above.

16. Liquidate zombie nouns.

So-called zombie nouns are abstract nouns that take the place of strong verbs. The tendency to turn strong verbs into abstract nouns accompanied by weak verbs (*is, do, make, have*) is one of the worst faults in modern writing. And the old civil rules were full of zombie nouns.

- **4(l); now 4(l)(3)**: *failure to make proof of service/failure to prove service.*

- **6(b); now 6(b)(1)(A):** *before the expiration of the period originally prescribed/before the original time . . . expires.*
- **7.1(b)(2):** *upon any change in the information that the statement requires/if any required information changes.*
- **11(c)(2)(A); now 11(c)(5)(A):** *for a violation of subdivision (b)(2)/for violating Rule 11(b)(2).*
- **13(a); now 13(a)(2)(B):** *the opposing party brought suit upon the claim/the opposing party sued on its claim.*
- **15(c)(3); now 15(c)(1)(C)(i):** *maintaining a defense on the merits/defending on the merits.*
- **26(g)(3):** *if . . . a certification is made in violation of the rule/if a certification violates this rule.*
- **30(b)(2); now 30(b)(3)(A):** *any party may arrange for a transcription to be made . . . of a deposition/any party may arrange to transcribe a deposition.*
- **30(e); now 30(e)(1):** *before completion of the deposition/before the deposition is completed.*
- **30(f)(2); now 30(f)(3):** *upon payment of reasonable charges therefor, the officer shall/when paid reasonable charges, the officer must.*
- **41(b):** *for failure of the plaintiff to prosecute/if the plaintiff fails to prosecute.*
- **45(a)(1)(C); now 45(a)(1)(A)(iii):** *give testimony/testify.*
- **47(a):** *conduct the examination of prospective jurors/examine prospective jurors.*
- **49(b); now 49(b)(1):** *make answers to the interrogatories/answer the questions.*

There are lots more where those came from.

17. Simplify inflated diction.

There's no need to belabor this point — and I've had my
say on it anyway.[11] Just ask yourself whether the plain words
on the right below in any way cheapen, dumb down, debase,
distort, oversimplify, or dull the new rules. Remember Walt
Whitman's line: "The art of art, the glory of expression . . . is
simplicity. Nothing is better than simplicity . . . ."[12]

- **4 (throughout):** *effect service/make service* or *serve.*
- **4(d)(2), last sentence; now 4(d)(2)(A):** *subsequently
  incurred/later incurred.*
- **4(d)(2)(B); now 4(d)(1)(G):** *dispatched/sent.*
- **8(b); now 8(b)(4):** *remainder/rest.*
- **9(a); now 9(a)(2):** *specific negative averment/specific
  denial.*
- **12(e):** *interposing a responsive pleading/filing a responsive pleading.*
- **15(b); now 15(b)(1):** *will be subserved/will aid.*
- **30(b)(4); now 30(b)(5)(C):** *concerning/about.*
- **30(e); now 30(e)(1)(B):** *reciting such changes/listing
  the changes.*
- **30(e); now 30(e)(2):** *append/attach.*
- **32(a)(3), last sentence; now 32(a)(5)(B):** *demon-
  strates/shows.*
- **32(d)(3)(C):** *propounding* [the question]/*submitting
  the question.*
- **32(d)(4):** *ascertained/known.*
- **36(b):** *will be subserved/would promote.*
- **37(a)(2)(B); now 37(a)(3)(C):** *the proponent of the
  question/the party asking a question.*
- **37(b), last sentence; now 37(b)(2)(C):** *in lieu of/in-
  stead of.*

---

[11] *See* Kimble, *Plain Words,* in *Lifting the Fog of Legalese* at 163–69.
[12] Preface to *Leaves of Grass.*

- **37(c)(2):** *thereafter/later.*
- **41(a)(2):** *deems/considers.*
- **49(b); now 49(b)(2):** *harmonious/consistent.*
- **62(d):** *procuring/obtaining.*
- **65(b); now 65(b)(2):** *be indorsed with the date/state the date.*

18. Banish *shall.*

The most telling indictment of most lawyers' drafting incompetence is that they fall apart over the most important words in the drafting lexicon — the words of authority, the words that are supposed to create a requirement or confer permission. The prime offender, as it has been for centuries, is *shall.* The word has been so corrupted by misuse that it has become inherently ambiguous. It should mean "must," but too often it's used to mean or interpreted to mean "should" or "may" — not to mention those instances in which, because no requirement *or* permission is intended, the simple present tense of the verb is called for. No wonder, then, that *Words and Phrases* online cites more than 1,775 appellate cases interpreting *shall.*[13]

But a remarkable thing happened in the mid-1990s: the Standing Committee on Rules of Practice and Procedure, which reviews and must approve the work of all five advisory committees on federal rules (civil, criminal, appellate, evidence, and bankruptcy), decided to abolish *shall.* The decision was given effect in 4.2 of Bryan Garner's *Guidelines for Drafting and Editing Court Rules*, published by the Administrative Office of the United States Courts in 1996. That pamphlet has guided all four restylings of the federal rules (in order, appellate, criminal, civil, and now evidence), as well as all new and amended rules.

---

[13] Search in Westlaw, Words–Phrases database, using the search "shall" (Feb. 5, 2017) (yielding 1,776 results — a number that will steadily keep rising).

If the wisdom of deep-sixing *shall* needs any testament, you'll find it in statistics from the old and new civil rules. Some of the numbers are rounded off because the counting can be tricky and because my purpose is not to be exact but just to give a good idea of *shall*'s sloppiness.

The old rules contained almost 500 *shall*s, not including those in rules that were deleted (such as Rule 86(b)–(d)). Of the 500, some 375 were converted to *must* in the new rules; 25% of the time, then, *shall* was not converted to its presumed meaning of "must."

There are five categories to consider.

First, *shall* was changed to a present-tense verb about 50 times. The conversion was easier in some cases than in others.

Old 2	New 2
There *shall be* one form of action to be known as "civil action".	There *is* one form of action — the civil action.

Old 27(a)(3)	New 27(a)(3)
(3) Order and Examination. . . . For the purpose of applying these rules to depositions for perpetuating testimony, each reference therein to the court in which the action is pending *shall be deemed to refer to* the court in which the petition for such deposition was filed.	**(3) *Order and Examination.*** . . . A reference in these rules to the court where an action is pending *means*, for purposes of this rule, the court where the petition for the deposition was filed.

Old 57	New 57
The procedure for obtaining a declaratory judgment pursuant to Title 28, U.S.C., § 2201, *shall be in accordance with* these rules	These rules *govern* the procedure for obtaining a declaratory judgment under 28 U.S.C. § 2201. . . .

Second, *shall* was twice changed to *will*. Example:

Old 27(a)(3)	New 27(a)(3)
(3) **Order and Examination.** . . . [T]he court . . . shall make an order . . . specifying . . . whether the depositions *shall* be taken upon oral examination or written interrogatories. . . .	(3) *Order and Examination.* . . . [T]he court must issue an order that . . . states whether the depositions *will* be taken orally or by written interrogatories. . . .

Third, *shall* was changed to *should* 14 times. Example:

Old 54(a)	New 54(a)
(a) **Definition; Form.** . . . A judgment *shall* not contain a recital of pleadings	(a) **Definition; Form.** . . . A judgment *should* not include recitals of pleadings . . . .

The fourth category is more complicated. *Shall* was converted to some kind of *may*-formulation about 25 times. But they fall into different patterns, different subcategories — four, in fact.

Pattern 1: a requirement was turned into mere permission. This happened five times that I found. Example:

Old 78	New 78
[E]ach district court *shall establish* regular times and places . . . at which motions requiring notice and hearing may be heard and disposed of	**(a) Providing a Regular Schedule for Oral Hearings.** A court *may establish* regular times and places for oral hearings on motions.

Pattern 2: the old rule used a clumsy *shall*-phrase to grant permission. This happened just once.

Old 71A(h)	New 71.1(h)(2)(C)
(h) Trial. . . . Each party *shall have the right to* object for valid cause to the appointment of any person as a commissioner or alternate.	(C) *Examining the Prospective Commissioners.* . . . The parties . . . for good cause *may* object to a prospective commissioner or alternate.

Pattern 3: the old rule used *shall . . . only* instead of *may . . . only* to create conditional permission. This happened at least four times. Example:

Old 16(e)	New 16(e)
(e) Pretrial Orders. . . . The order following a final pretrial conference *shall* be modified *only* to prevent manifest injustice.	**(e) Final Pretrial Conference and Orders.** . . . The court *may* modify the order issued after a final pretrial conference *only* to prevent manifest injustice.

Pattern 4: the old rule used *shall not* or *no _____ shall* to create a prohibition, usually a qualified prohibition. Note that a qualified prohibition is, in effect, conditional permission. What you can't do in certain circumstances you presumably can do if the circumstances don't exist. This pattern occurred more than 15 times. Examples:

Old 23.1	New 23.1(c)
. . . The [derivative] action *shall not* be dismissed or compromised *without* the approval of the court	(c) *Settlement, Dismissal, and Compromise.* A derivative action *may* be settled, voluntarily dismissed, or compromised *only* with the court's approval. . . .

Old 17(a)	New 17(a)(3)
(a) **Real Party in Interest.** . . . No action *shall* be dismissed on the ground that it is not prosecuted in the name of the real party in interest *until* a reasonable time has been allowed after objection for ratification of commencement of the action by, or joinder or substitution of, the real party in interest	(3) *Joinder of the Real Party in Interest.* The court *may not* dismiss an action for failure to prosecute in the name of the real party in interest *until,* after an objection, a reasonable time has been allowed for the real party in interest to ratify, join, or be substituted into the action. . . .

Old 65(a)(1)	New 65(a)(1)
(1) **Notice.** *No* preliminary injunction *shall* be issued *without* notice to the adverse party.	(1) *Notice.* The court *may* issue a preliminary injunction *only* on notice to the adverse party.

Of course, *shall* should never be used to grant permission; that calls for *may*. For conditional permission, *may . . . only* is usually the logical choice. To deny permission, the drafter may either create a prohibition with *must not* or use *may not*; they typically come out to the same thing. Just be careful that *may not* can't plausibly be read as "might not."

Returning to our five main categories, we come to our fifth and last one: almost 35 times, a rule was tightened and transformed in a way that eliminated *shall* altogether. Examples:

Old 30(b)(5)	New 30(b)(2)
(5) The notice to a party deponent may be accompanied by a request made in compliance with Rule 34 for the production of documents and tangible things at the taking of the deposition. The procedure of Rule 34 *shall* apply to the request.	(2) *Producing Documents.* . . . The notice to a party deponent may be accompanied by a request under Rule 34 to produce documents and tangible things at the deposition.

Old 79(a)	New 79(a)(3)
(a) Civil Docket. . . . These [docket] entries *shall* be brief but shall show the nature of each paper filed	(3) *Contents of Entries; Jury Trial Demanded.* Each [docket] entry must briefly show the nature of the paper filed . . . .

Here again are the overall totals for *shall*s that were not converted to *must* in the civil rules: 50 present-tense verbs, 2 *will*s, 14 *should*s, 25 *may*-formulations, and 35 disappearances through tightening.

Now, after all that, an incredible postscript. When the restyled rules took effect on December 1, 2007, they gloriously contained not a single *shall*. But that changed on December 1, 2010. One *shall* was reintroduced.

Before restyling, the all-important rule on summary judgment, Rule 56(c), said that the judgment *shall be rendered . . . if . . . there is no genuine issue as to any material fact. . . .* The restyled rule changed the *shall* to *should*. After the restyling, the Advisory Committee decided to amend the substance of Rule 56, and a battle ensued over whether the original *shall* meant "must" or "should."[14] And because the Advisory Committee could not decide on the meaning, they reinstated *shall* — while at the same time acknowledging that it is "inherently ambiguous."[15]

What a classic lesson in why *shall* should never appear in a legal document. It *is* inherently ambiguous, and ambiguity (not to be confused with vagueness) is the worst sin in legal drafting.[16]

19. Above all, avoid hardcore legalese.

We come at last to the kind of talk and writing that has brought endless ridicule on our profession — and rightly so.[17] There is no excuse for it. Thus, the new rules have done away with *pursuant to*. They have done away with *provided that* (provisos). They have done away with 500 — no, 499 — *shall*s. They don't use *such* when it means "a" or "the." They don't use *hereof* or *therefor* or *wherein*. In fact, the new rules have banished all the *here-*, *there-*, and *where-* words, with one painful exception. Rules 59(a)(1)(A) & (B) refer to "any reason for which a new trial [or rehearing] has heretofore been granted . . . in federal court." Can you guess why the Advisory Committee left these *heretofore*s? Because, here again, they could not decide whether it meant "up until 1937," when the rules were originally drafted, or "up until now," when a judge is applying the rules. And if that isn't

---

[14] *See* Mark R. Kravitz, *Report of Advisory Committee on Rules of Civil Procedure* 215–33 (May 8, 2009), http://www.uscourts.gov/rules-policies /archives/committee-reports/advisory-committee-rules-civil-procedure -May-2009 (summarizing the divided comments from the public).

[15] *Id.* at 20, 21.

[16] *See* Kimble, *How to Mangle Court Rules and Jury Instructions*, in *Lifting the Fog of Legalese* at 105, 119–21 (distinguishing between vagueness and ambiguity).

[17] *See* Kimble, *Lifting the Fog of Legalese* at app. 1 (quoting centuries of criticism).

another perfect example of the pseudo-precision of legalese, I don't know what is.

A few final examples from the old and new rules:

Old 4(l)	New 4(l)(1)
(l) Proof of Service. If service is not waived, the person effecting service shall make proof *thereof* to the court. If service is made by a person other than a United States marshal or deputy United States marshal, the person shall make affidavit *thereof*. . . .	**(l) Proving Service.** (1) *Affidavit Required.* Unless service is waived, proof of service must be made to the court. Except for service by a United States marshal or deputy marshal, proof must be by the server's affidavit.

Old 12(g)	New 12(g)(1)
(g) Consolidation of Defenses in Motion. A party who makes a motion under this rule may join with it any other motions *herein* provided for and then available to the party. . . .	**(g) Joining Motions.** (1) *Right to Join.* A motion under this rule may be joined with any other motion allowed by this rule.

Old 37(b)(2)	New 37(b)(2)

(2) Sanctions by Court in Which Action Is Pending. . . . [T]he court in which the action is pending may make *such* orders in regard to the failure [to obey certain orders] as are just, and among others the following:
 	
     .   .   .
	(2) *Sanctions in the District Where the Action Is Pending.*
	   (A) *For Not Obeying a Discovery Order.* . . . [T]he court where the action is pending may issue further just orders. They may include the following:
	
	     . . .

Old 37(b)(2)	New 37(b)(2)
(E) Where a party has failed to comply with an order under Rule 35(a) requiring that party to produce another for examination, *such* orders as are listed in paragraphs (A), (B), and (C) of this subdivision, unless the party failing to comply shows that that party is unable to produce *such* person for examination. In lieu of any of the *foregoing* orders or in addition *thereto*, the court shall	(B) *For Not Producing a Person for Examination.* If a party fails to comply with an order under Rule 35(a) requiring it to produce another person for examination, the court may issue any of the orders listed in Rule 37(b)(2)(A)(i)–(vi), unless the disobedient party shows that it cannot produce the other person. (C) *Payment of Expenses.* Instead of or in addition to the orders above, the court must . . . .

Old 49(a)	New 49(a)(2)
(a) **Special Verdicts.** . . . The court shall give to the jury *such* explanation and instruction concerning the matter thus submitted as may be necessary to enable the jury to make its findings upon each issue. . . .	(2) *Instructions.* The court must give the instructions and explanations necessary to enable the jury to make its findings on each submitted issue.

Old 52(a)	New 52(a)(1)
(a) **Effect.** In all actions tried upon the facts without a jury or with an advisory jury, the court shall find the facts specially and state separately its conclusions of law *thereon*, and judgment shall be entered *pursuant to* Rule 58	(a) **Findings and Conclusions.** (1) *In General.* In an action tried on the facts without a jury or with an advisory jury, the court must find the facts specially and state its conclusions of law separately. . . . Judgment must be entered under Rule 58.

Let's end where we began. The restyled civil rules are a dramatic improvement on the old rules. The new rules will be far easier for law students to learn and for lawyers and judges to use. If any inadvertent substantive changes were made, they can be fixed. And people who resisted this conversion probably did not appreciate how poorly drafted the old rules were, how they perpetuated the serious deficiencies that have plagued us for so long, how we should not be forever stuck in time, and how the new rules mark a long stride forward for legal writing and professional competence — not to mention the practice of law.

A Drafting Example from the New Federal Rules of Evidence

The next four essays appeared in the Michigan Bar Journal's *Plain Language column just after the restyled Federal Rules of Evidence were published for comment, in August 2009. Naturally, what the essays refer to as "current rules" and "restyled rules" are now the old rules and the new rules. The new rules took effect on December 1, 2011.*

There's a new milestone on the long road to better legal writing. On June 1 [2009], the Standing Committee on Rules of Practice and Procedure approved for publication the "restyled" Federal Rules of Evidence. As drafting consultant, I began redrafting the rules in mid-2006, and in April the Advisory Committee on Evidence Rules approved the last set for transmittal to the Standing Committee.

The goal has been to make the rules clearer, more consistent, and more readable — all without changing their meaning. No small assignment, and as you can imagine, the Advisory Committee scrutinized every word, looking for possible substantive change. The careful, systematic, three-year process is summarized by Judge Robert Hinkle, Chair of the Advisory Committee, in a report that's available by searching Google for "Advisory Committee on Rules of Evidence, April 2009." The report includes side-by-side versions of the current and restyled rules.

Of course, the work is not done. No doubt the public comments will produce any number of changes. And the final version must then be approved by the Standing Committee (again), the Judicial Conference of the United States, the Supreme Court, and Congress. The track record, though, is good: this is the fourth set of federal rules to be restyled. The Rules of Appellate Procedure took effect in 1998, the Rules of Criminal Procedure in 2002, and the Rules of Civil Procedure in 2007.

During the comment period for the civil rules, I wrote two Plain Language columns (December 2004 and January 2005) showing side-by-side examples of several old and new rules, and simply asked you readers to be the judge. This time, I'll do more. In each of four separate essays, I'll look in detail at one rule and describe in slightly enlarged footnotes some of its drafting deficiencies; then offer the restyled rule with comments on the main differences; and then set them side by side at the end. (The restyled rules are shorter, although their improved structure makes that less apparent in the narrow side-by-side columns.)

Nobody would claim that the restyled rules are perfect; on a project like this, you can always find pieces that could have been — and perhaps still will be — improved. Naturally, though, I do think that the new rules are far better. But see what you think. Here's the first of four.

Current Rule 609(a)–(b)
Impeachment by Evidence of Conviction of Crime

(a) **General Rule.** For the purpose of[1] attacking the character for truthfulness of a witness,[2]

Drafting Deficiencies

1. *For the purpose of* is a multiword preposition. Make it *To attack*.
2. An unnecessary prepositional phrase. Make it *a witness's character*.

(1)[3] evidence that a witness other than an accused has been convicted of a crime shall[4] be admitted, subject to Rule 403, if the crime was punishable by death or imprisonment in excess of[5] one year[6] under the law under which the witness was convicted,[7] and evidence that an accused has been convicted of such[8] a crime[9] shall be admitted if the court determines that[10] the probative value of admitting this evidence outweighs its prejudicial effect to the accused;[11] and

(2) evidence that any witness has been convicted of a crime shall be admitted regardless of the punishment, if it readily[12] can be determined that[13] establishing the

---

3. Two structural points. (1) Without digging, it's hard to tell what the point of distinction is between this first paragraph and the second one; the restyled rule makes that clear at the beginning of each paragraph. (2) This dense first paragraph contains two possibilities that should be broken down.
4. *Shall* has become inherently ambiguous (among other disadvantages). The restyled rules use *must* for required actions.
5. A stuffy way of saying *for more than*.
6. Note the miscue: *in excess of one year* modifies *imprisonment* but not *death*. To avoid the miscue, insert *by* before *imprisonment*.
7. Arguably, it's obvious what law we're talking about. But the restyled rule at least shortens this clumsy phrasing to *in the convicting jurisdiction*.
8. A lot hangs on the word *such*. It avoids repetition, but it would be easy to blow past.
9. Note the repetition of *evidence that . . . has been convicted of . . . a crime* from the first part of this paragraph.
10. There's no such *the court determines that* in, for instance, Rule 403. The restyled rule omits it.
11. An unnecessary prepositional phrase. Of course we're talking about the effect on the accused. Strike *to the accused*.
12. The adverb should normally split the verb phrase. Whether to put it after the first or second of two auxiliary verbs can be tricky, but I'd say *readily* belongs after *be*.
13. Here, the *can be determined that* language needs to stay in order to keep the idea of "readily." But why is it passive?

elements of the crime required proof or admission[14] of
an act of dishonesty[15] or false statement by the witness.[16]

(b) Time Limit.[17] Evidence of a conviction under this
rule[18] is not admissible if a period of[19] more than[20] ten years has
elapsed since the date of[21] the conviction or of the release of the
witness[22] from the confinement imposed for that conviction,[23]
whichever is the later date, unless[24] the court determines, in the
interests of justice, that[25] the probative value of the conviction
supported by specific facts and circumstances substantially
outweighs its prejudicial effect.[26] However,[27] evidence of
a conviction more than 10[28] years old as calculated herein,[29]

---

14. Prefer the *-ing* forms — *proving* and *admitting* — to the nouns with
    of.
15. Another unnecessary prepositional phrase. Make it *a dishonest act*.
16. The language beginning with *proof* is a syntactic muddle. We're talk-
    ing about the witness's admitting something, but not the witness's
    proving something.
17. Not an informative heading. The restyled heading makes it immedi-
    ately clear when this part applies.
18. Of course we're talking about a conviction under this rule. Strike *un-
    der this rule*.
19. Strike *a period of*.
20. Note the inconsistency with *in excess of* in (a)(1).
21. Strike *the date of*.
22. Make it *the witness's conviction or release*.
23. To this point, the sentence uses nine prepositional phrases. The re-
    styled rule uses three.
24. Note the double negative: *is not admissible . . . unless*. Make it *is ad-
    missible only if*.
25. Again, strike *the court determines . . . that*, along with *in the interests
    of justice*. The latter is a needless intensifier anyway.
26. This is a 72-word sentence.
27. Start sentences with *But*, not *However*. What's more, this sentence
    actually contains a second condition to using the evidence. The rule
    should be structured to show that the evidence is allowed only if two
    conditions are met.
28. The previous sentence spells out *ten*.
29. Strike *as calculated herein*. Also, the comma needs a paired comma
    after *old*.

is not admissible unless[30] the proponent gives to the adverse party sufficient advance[31] written notice of intent to use such evidence[32] to provide the adverse party with a fair opportunity to contest the use of such evidence.[33]

Now for the proposed new rule. Most of the changes are explained by my comments on the current rule. I'll just make three salient points. First, the current rule contains 262 words; the new one contains 204, or 22% fewer. Second, the new rule is structured in a way that reflects the content much more clearly. Third, the new rule improves the formatting with progressive indents for the subparts and hanging indents (aligned on the left) within each subpart.

Restyled Rule 609(a)–(b)
Impeachment by Evidence of a Criminal Conviction
[later modified slightly, before final approval]

(a) **In General.** The following rules apply to attacking a witness's character for truthfulness by evidence of a criminal conviction:

    (1) for a crime that, in the convicting jurisdiction, was punishable by death or by imprisonment for more than one year, the evidence:

        (A) must be admitted, subject to Rule 403, if the witness is not a defendant in a criminal case; and

        (B) must be admitted if the witness is a defendant in a criminal case and the probative value of the evidence outweighs its prejudicial effect; and

---

30. Another double negative.
31. Isn't notice always in advance? At any rate, here it certainly has to be.
32. Try a pronoun — *it* — instead of *such evidence*.
33. Try another pronoun — *its* — as in *its use*.

(2) for any crime regardless of the punishment, the evidence must be admitted if the court can readily determine that establishing the elements of the crime required proving — or the witness's admitting — a dishonest act or false statement.

(b) Limit on Using the Evidence After 10 Years. This subdivision (b) applies if more than 10 years have passed since the witness's conviction or release from confinement for the conviction, whichever is later. Evidence of the conviction is admissible only if:

(1) its probative value, supported by specific facts and circumstances, substantially outweighs its prejudicial effect; and

(2) the proponent gives an adverse party reasonable written notice of the intent to use it so that the party has a fair opportunity to contest its use.

Old Rule 609(a)–(b)	Restyled Rule 609(a)–(b)
Impeachment by Evidence of Conviction of Crime	**Impeachment by Evidence of a Criminal Conviction** [modified slightly before final approval]
(a) **General Rule.** For the purpose of attacking the character for truthfulness of a witness,	(a) **In General.** The following rules apply to attacking a witness's character for truthfulness by evidence of a criminal conviction:
(1) evidence that a witness other than an accused has been convicted of a crime shall be admitted, subject to Rule 403, if the crime was punishable by death or imprisonment in excess of one year under the law under which the witness was convicted, and evidence that an accused has been convicted of such a crime shall be admitted if the court determines that the probative value of admitting this evidence outweighs its prejudicial effect to the accused; and	(1) for a crime that, in the convicting jurisdiction, was punishable by death or by imprisonment for more than one year, the evidence:
	(A) must be admitted, subject to Rule 403, if the witness is not a defendant in a criminal case; and
	(B) must be admitted if the witness is a defendant in a criminal case and the probative value of the evidence outweighs its prejudicial effect; and

(2) evidence that any witness has been convicted of a crime shall be admitted regardless of the punishment, if it readily can be determined that establishing the elements of the crime required proof or admission of an act of dishonesty or false statement by the witness.

(b) Time Limit. Evidence of a conviction under this rule is not admissible if a period of more than ten years has elapsed since the date of the conviction or of the release of the witness from the confinement imposed for that conviction, whichever is the later date, unless the court determines, in the interests of justice, that the probative value of the conviction supported by specific facts and circumstances substantially outweighs its prejudicial effect. However, evidence of a conviction more than 10 years old as calculated herein, is not admissible unless the proponent gives to the adverse party sufficient advance written notice of intent to use such evidence to provide the adverse party with a fair opportunity to contest the use of such evidence.

(2) for any crime regardless of the punishment, the evidence must be admitted if the court can readily determine that establishing the elements of the crime required proving — or the witness's admitting — a dishonest act or false statement.

(b) Limit on Using the Evidence After 10 Years. This subdivision (b) applies if more than 10 years have passed since the witness's conviction or release from confinement for the conviction, whichever is later. Evidence of the conviction is admissible only if:

(1) its probative value, supported by specific facts and circumstances, substantially outweighs its prejudicial effect; and

(2) the proponent gives an adverse party reasonable written notice of the intent to use it so that the party has a fair opportunity to contest its use.

Another Example from the
New Federal Rules of Evidence

In the introductory essay to his 2009 book *Garner on Language and Writing*, Bryan Garner offers a sobering indictment: "a supermajority of lawyers — even law professors — grossly overestimate their writing skills, and underestimate the importance of those skills." That's the view of the preeminent authority on the subject. And what he says goes double for the category of legal writing that we call drafting—statutes, rules, contracts, wills, and the like.

So why has most legal drafting been so bad for so long? I posed that same question earlier in the *Lessons in Drafting* essay (pages 57–59) and offered five reasons: (1) law schools have by and large failed to teach drafting; (2) most lawyers don't fill the void through self-education, but rather tend to just copy the lumbering old forms; (3) young lawyers may have to "learn" drafting at the hands of older lawyers who never learned the skill themselves but who think their expertise in a particular field makes them adept drafters; (4) lawyers typically believe they should draft for judges rather than front-end users like clients, the public, and administrators; and (5) transactional lawyers seem more indifferent to the skill of drafting than litigators are to the skill of analytical and persuasive writing.

Let me add another reason, a cousin to #2: with rare exceptions, the apparent models that law students and lawyers have to work with are poorly drafted. Think of the Uniform Commercial Code, the United States Code, the Code of Federal Regulations, the Federal Rules of Civil Procedure until late 2007, most state statutes and regulations and court rules, most model jury instructions, municipal ordinances by the tens of thousands—the entire bunch. So pervasive is the old style of drafting that, unless we've somehow seen the light, we can't help but regard it as perfectly normal and good, and we can't help but internalize it.

But a remarkable thing happened in the early 1990s: the Standing Committee on (Federal) Rules of Practice and Procedure saw the light. The Committee recognized that the federal court rules were in a bad way, and it undertook the daunting task of "restyling" them set by set. It created a Style Subcommittee, which enlisted the help of a drafting consultant (first Bryan Garner, then me). The consultant prepared the drafts; they were meticulously reviewed by the Style Subcommittee and by the Advisory Committee for each set of rules; they were approved by the Supreme Court; and we now have new Federal Rules of Appellate Procedure (1998), Criminal Procedure (2002), and Civil Procedure (2007), and proposed new Federal Rules of Evidence.

I think it's fair to say that the appellate, criminal, and civil restylings have been remarkably successful. Everyone seems to agree that the new rules are much clearer and more consistent, and since they took effect, only a few corrections have been needed — out of three complete rewrites. Still, during the public-comment periods, we heard from some quarters that "mere" restyling was not worth the effort or that restyling was a solution in search of a problem or that some other such objection loomed large. Never mind that the old rules were riddled with inconsistencies, ambiguities, disorganization, poor formatting, clumps of unbroken text, uninformative headings, unwieldy sentences, verbosity, repetition, abstractitis, unnecessary cross-references, multiple negatives, inflated diction, and legalese. Never mind that the old rules were a professional embarrassment. Never mind that those who would dismiss the restylings as unneeded must (as most lawyers do) have little regard for good drafting — or ease of reading. Never mind that they'd be willing to consign us to the old models forever.

So now the evidence rules have been restyled. In the previous essay, I offered an example — a current rule with detailed comments, followed by the restyled rule. I'll do the same thing below. Try to put yourself in the place of a law student reading the current rule for the first time. And remember that just about all the evidence rules — certainly those of any length — can be given the same treatment.

Current Rule 612
Writing Used to Refresh Memory[1]

Except as otherwise provided in criminal proceedings by section 3500 of title 18, United States Code,[2] if a witness uses a writing to refresh memory for the purpose of[3] testifying, either —[4]

    (1) while testifying, or

    (2) before testifying, if the court in its discretion[5] determines[6] it[7] is necessary in the interests of justice,

---

Drafting Deficiencies

1. Whose memory? Also, just glance at the rule. How discouraging is it to see such a stretch of unbroken text?
2. Wordy phrasing with a clunky citation. Note the three prepositional phrases. The restyled rule uses one.
3. *For the purpose of* is a multiword preposition. It should usually be replaced with *to*. Here it isn't needed at all. The purpose is clear from what follows.
4. Why use a dash, rather than a colon, to introduce a vertical list? What's more, the list appears midsentence — not the best practice. Some drafting experts allow it, but our guidelines for federal rules require that lists be placed at the end of the sentence. *See* Bryan A. Garner, *Guidelines for Drafting and Editing Court Rules* 3.3(B) (Admin. Office U.S. Courts 1996), available by Googling the title.
5. Strike *in its discretion*. It's as useless as can be.
6. Add *that* after *determines*. Most verbs need *that* to smoothly introduce a following clause.
7. A classic. What does *it* refer to? What's the antecedent? Actually, the reference is forward, but not to any identifiable noun. *It* refers loosely to what a party is entitled to.

an adverse party is entitled to have the writing produced at the hearing, to inspect it, to cross-examine the witness thereon,[8] and to introduce in evidence those portions[9] which[10] relate to the testimony of the witness.[11] If it is claimed[12] that the writing contains matters[13] not related to the subject matter of the testimony[14] the court shall[15] examine the writing in camera, excise[16] any portions not so related,[17] and order delivery of[18] the remainder[19] to the party entitled thereto.[20] Any portion withheld[21] over objections[22] shall be preserved and made available to the appellate court in the event of an appeal.[23] If a writing is not produced or

---

8. Legalese.
9. As a rule, draft in the singular to avoid ambiguity. What if the adverse party wants to introduce just one portion? Sure, the plural probably covers that here, but other contexts might not be as clear. And by convention the singular includes the plural.
10. Use *that* when the relative pronoun introduces a restrictive clause, one that's essential to the basic meaning.
11. An unnecessary prepositional phrase. Make it *the witness's testimony*.
12. Why is this passive? Quick — who is claiming?
13. Is one matter enough? See note 9.
14. A lot of words for *unrelated matter*. We know that *unrelated* means unrelated to the testimony. Also, put a comma after *testimony*, which ends the long subordinate clause. Punctuation 101.
15. Make it *must*. Likewise in the next use (after *objections*) and the last use (after *the order*). And good riddance to the inherently ambiguous *shall*.
16. How about *delete*?
17. How about *unrelated portion*?
18. Even the passive voice — *be delivered* — is preferable to the zombie noun *delivery* with *of*. Better a verb than an abstract noun. See the February 2007 column.
19. How about *rest*?
20. Legalese.
21. Withheld by whom? See the miscue? Withheld by the judge or by whoever produces the writing? Using the same term as in the previous sentence — *excise[d]* or *delete[d]* — would make the meaning immediately clear. Consistency is the cardinal rule of drafting.
22. Is one objection enough?
23. A lot of words for *must be preserved for the record*.

delivered pursuant to[24] order[25] under this rule,[26] the court shall[27] make any order justice requires,[28] except that in criminal cases when the prosecution elects not to[29] comply, the order shall be one striking the testimony or, if the court in its discretion[30] determines that the interests of justice so require, declaring a mistrial.[31]

The restyled version below, besides fixing 30-odd drafting deficiencies, uses 41 fewer words, breaks the rule down into subdivisions, and converts four long sentences to six that are shorter by almost half.

Restyled Rule 612
Writing Used to Refresh a Witness's Memory
[later modified slightly, before final approval]

(a) **Scope.** This rule gives an adverse party certain options when a witness uses a writing to refresh memory:

    (1) while testifying; or

    (2) before testifying, if the court decides that justice requires a party to have those options.

(b) **Adverse Party's Options; Deleting Unrelated Matter.** Unless 18 U.S.C. § 3500 provides otherwise in a criminal case, an adverse party is entitled to have the writing produced at the hearing, to inspect it, to cross-examine the witness about it, and to introduce in evidence any portion that relates to the witness's

---

24. Legalese.
25. Another miscue: *pursuant to order* modifies *delivered*, but not *produced*. Make it *is not produced or is not delivered as ordered*.
26. Strike *under this rule* as entirely obvious.
27. Should this be *may*? That's the kind of trouble *shall* causes.
28. Insert a period and start a new sentence with *But*. That breaks up a 60-word sentence.
29. How about *does not*?
30. Again, strike *in its discretion*.
31. Everything beginning with *the order* is indirect and rather clumsy. It should simply say that "the court must do X or Y."

testimony. If the producing party claims that the writing includes unrelated matter, the court must examine
the writing in camera, delete any unrelated portion, and
order that the rest be delivered to the adverse party.
Any portion deleted over objection must be preserved
for the record.

(c) **Failure to Produce or Deliver.** If a writing is not
produced or is not delivered as ordered, the court may
issue any appropriate order. But if the prosecution does
not comply in a criminal case, the court must strike the
witness's testimony or — if justice so requires — declare a mistrial.

Old Rule 612	Restyled Rule 612
Writing Used to Refresh Memory	**Writing Used to Refresh a Witness's Memory** [modified slightly before final approval]
Except as otherwise provided in criminal proceedings by section 3500 of title 18, United States Code, if a witness uses a writing to refresh memory for the purpose of testifying, either — (1) while testifying, or (2) before testifying, if the court in its discretion determines it is necessary in the interests of justice, an adverse party is entitled to have the writing produced at the hearing, to inspect it, to cross-examine the witness thereon, and to introduce in evidence those portions which relate to the testimony of the witness. If it is claimed that the writing contains matters not related to the subject matter of the testimony the court shall examine the writing in camera, excise any portions not so related, and order delivery of the remainder to the party entitled thereto. Any portion withheld over objections shall be preserved and made available to the appellate court in the event of an appeal. If a writing is not	**(a) Scope.** This rule gives an adverse party certain options when a witness uses a writing to refresh memory: (1) while testifying; or (2) before testifying, if the court decides that justice requires a party to have those options. **(b) Adverse Party's Options; Deleting Unrelated Matter.** Unless 18 U.S.C. § 3500 provides otherwise in a criminal case, an adverse party is entitled to have the writing produced at the hearing, to inspect it, to cross-examine the witness about it, and to introduce in evidence any portion that relates to the witness's testimony. If the producing party claims that the writing includes unrelated matter, the court must examine the writing in camera, delete any unrelated portion, and order

produced or delivered pursuant to order under this rule, the court shall make any order justice requires, except that in criminal cases when the prosecution elects not to comply, the order shall be one striking the testimony or, if the court in its discretion determines that the interests of justice so require, declaring a mistrial.

that the rest be delivered to the adverse party. Any portion deleted over objection must be preserved for the record.

(c) **Failure to Produce or Deliver.** If a writing is not produced or is not delivered as ordered, the court may issue any appropriate order. But if the prosecution does not comply in a criminal case, the court must strike the witness's testimony or — if justice so requires — declare a mistrial.

Still Another Example from the New Federal Rules of Evidence

In August [2009], after a three-year project, the completely "restyled" Federal Rules of Evidence were published for comment. The project's goal was to redraft the rules in a modern, plain-language style — making them clearer, more consistent, and more readable — without changing their substantive meaning. An even broader goal has been to make the drafting style consistent throughout all the federal rules. Remember that three other sets of rules — Appellate, Criminal, and Civil Procedure — have already been redrafted. In fact, the work began more than 15 years ago.

The example below, my third evidence example, is shorter than those in the two previous essays, so I won't be able to identify as many deficiencies. I noted 33 in the first example and 31 in the second; this time, only 18, although they include a serious ambiguity. See whether you can spot it.

Current Rule 806
Attacking and Supporting Credibility of Declarant[1]

When a hearsay statement, or a statement defined[2] in Rule 801(d)(2)(C), (D), or (E), has been admitted in evidence, the credibility of the declarant[3] may be attacked, and if attacked may be supported,[4] by any evidence which[5] would be admissible for those purposes if declarant[6] had testified as a witness. Evidence of a statement or conduct by the declarant[7] at any time, inconsistent[8] with the declarant's

Drafting Deficiencies

1. An unnecessary prepositional phrase. Make it *the Declarant's Credibility.*
2. There's no definition in Rule 801(d)(2)(C), (D), or (E).
3. Again, make it *the declarant's credibility.*
4. A lot of words for *and then supported.*
5. Use *that*, not *which*, when the relative pronoun introduces a so-called restrictive clause, one that doesn't simply provide supplemental information but rather is essential to convey the basic meaning. Typically, *which* is correct only if you can insert a comma before it, setting off the clause.
6. Why is it *the declarant* everywhere else? This may seem like a small point, but consistency is the first rule of drafting, and the drafter who makes small missteps is headed for larger ones.
7. Another unnecessary prepositional phrase. Make it *the declarant's statement or conduct.*
8. *At any time, inconsistent* is rather clumsy, and the punctuation doesn't save it. *Inconsistent* belongs with *statement or conduct.* We know that *inconsistent* means inconsistent with the statement admitted in evidence, so the *with*-phrase after *inconsistent* can go. And the paired commas after *time* and *statement* aren't standard; they were probably inserted as a makeshift fix for the disruption caused by *at any time.*

hearsay statement,[9] is[10] not subject to any requirement[11] that the declarant may[12] have been afforded[13] an opportunity to deny or explain.[14] If the party against whom a hearsay statement[15] has been admitted[16] calls the declarant as a witness, the party is entitled to[17] examine the declarant on the statement as if under[18] cross-examination.

Note some of the more obvious improvements in the restyled rule that follows. It uses dashes, rather than commas, for the longish midsentence alternative in the first sentence. It smooths out the second sentence and states the meaning more directly. (The parallel structure of *regardless of when . . . or whether* helps considerably.) It's a little tighter overall. And most importantly, it fixes the ambiguity described in notes 9 and 15. The sentences are longer on average than I'd like (33 words), but the other restyled rules do better.

---

9. A critical ambiguity crops up here. The previous sentence talks about two statements: (1) a hearsay statement and (2) a statement described in Rule 801(d)(2). But the 801(d)(2) statement is, by the very terms of 801(d), "not hearsay." So when this second sentence of 806 refers to a "hearsay statement," it seems to be referring only to the first "statement" in the previous sentence — a hearsay statement — and not an 801(d)(2) statement. Was that limitation intended?

10. Another thing that makes this sentence unwieldy: the verb, *is*, is too far from the subject, *evidence*.

11. Why is this nonrequirement stated so indirectly? Why not *the court may admit evidence of . . . even if . . .* ? The restyled rule does it a little differently, but along the same lines.

12. Strike *may*. This whole verb phrase needs reworking.

13. How about *given*?

14. Deny or explain what? Readers are brought up short. Apparently, the drafters didn't want to use the pronoun *it*, sensing that the antecedent would be unclear, or to add *the inconsistent statement or conduct*. Trapped with no way out.

15. The ambiguity deepens. By again using *hearsay statement*, the sentence seems to invoke only the first "statement" in the first sentence. See note 9.

16. No need to use the present perfect tense. Make it *was admitted*.

17. Replace *is entitled to* with *may*.

18. Wouldn't *on* be more idiomatic — *as if on cross-examination*?

Restyled Rule 806
Attacking and Supporting the Declarant's Credibility

When a hearsay statement — or a statement described in Rule 801(d)(2)(C), (D), or (E) — has been admitted in evidence, the declarant's credibility may be attacked, and then supported, by any evidence that would be admissible for those purposes if the declarant had testified as a witness. The court may admit evidence of the declarant's inconsistent statement or conduct, regardless of when it occurred or whether the declarant had an opportunity to explain or deny it. If the party against whom the statement was admitted calls the declarant as a witness, the party may examine the declarant on the statement as if on cross-examination.

Old Rule 806	Restyled Rule 806
Attacking and Supporting Credibility of Declarant	**Attacking and Supporting the Declarant's Credibility**
When a hearsay statement, or a statement defined in Rule 801(d)(2)(C), (D), or (E), has been admitted in evidence, the credibility of the declarant may be attacked, and if attacked may be supported, by any evidence which would be admissible for those purposes if declarant had testified as a witness. Evidence of a statement or conduct by the declarant at any time, inconsistent with the declarant's hearsay statement, is not subject to any requirement that the declarant may have been afforded an opportunity to deny or explain. If the party against whom a hearsay statement has been admitted calls the declarant as a witness, the party is entitled to examine the declarant on the statement as if under cross-examination.	When a hearsay statement — or a statement described in Rule 801(d)(2)(C), (D), or (E) — has been admitted in evidence, the declarant's credibility may be attacked, and then supported, by any evidence that would be admissible for those purposes if the declarant had testified as a witness. The court may admit evidence of the declarant's inconsistent statement or conduct, regardless of when it occurred or whether the declarant had an opportunity to explain or deny it. If the party against whom the statement was admitted calls the declarant as a witness, the party may examine the declarant on the statement as if on cross-examination.

One Last Example from the New Federal Rules of Evidence

This is the fourth and final essay on drafting examples from the restyled Federal Rules of Evidence. I have tried to illustrate the improvement by pulling out a few current rules, briefly describing their deficiencies, and showing you the restyled rules for comparison. Thus, I noted 33 deficiencies in Rule 609(a)–(b), 31 in Rule 612, and 18 in Rule 806, and below I'll note 28 in Rule 404(a). Perhaps that's enough to make the case.

Before looking at 404(a), I'd like to do something different — and possibly surprising. I'd like to acknowledge some drafting flaws in the restyled rules. As I said in the first of these essays, nobody would claim that the restyled rules are perfect; you can always go back and find ways to improve on the improvements. Of course, any large-scale project like this will involve countless decisions and many compromises. And on some matters, the Advisory Committee on Evidence Rules had to decide whether to follow the best drafting practices in the face of other considerations.

So what could have been fixed in an ideal world, if we had been starting from scratch? We might have changed the structure of various restyled rules in several ways.

For one thing, the numbering in Rules 803 and 902 is unlike the numbering in the other restyled rules: as in the two current rules, 803 and 902 follow the rule number with another number — 803(6), for instance. To achieve consistency, that could have been 803(a)(6) or (b)(6), although creating the new (a) or (b) might have required a little artfulness.

For another thing, those same two rules, along with 801(d), 804(b), and 901(b), use a hybrid format. Technically,

119

they are set up as items in a list, but they look like subparts with headings. (Compare, for instance, Rule 807: it has two subparts, two subdivisions, each with a heading, and then a list without headings in subdivision (a). That's the norm in the restyled rules — the items in a list do not carry headings.) But the anomaly may be justifiable because the "lists" in those five rules are so long and complicated.

Another formatting anomaly: Rule 502 has a freestanding, undesignated, uncitable piece at the beginning, before the first subdivision. It should have been subdivision (a), but the Advisory Committee had reason to not adjust the version passed by Congress.

Finally, in Rule 801(d)(2), Rule 803(5), (6), (7), (8), (18), and (22), and Rule 804(a), you'll find so-called dangling text — a sentence that follows an enumerated vertical list. Although some drafting experts find this practice unobjectionable and even useful, the guidelines for drafting federal rules discourage it.

So much for structural imperfections — which hardly diminish the great leap forward taken by the restyled rules. And no doubt the public comments will lead to a number of further improvements in wording. Meanwhile, let's take up our last example.

Current Rule 404(a)
Character Evidence Not Admissible
to Prove Conduct;[1] Exceptions; Other Crimes

(a) **Character evidence generally.** Evidence of a person's character or a[2] trait of character[3] is not admissible for the purpose of[4] proving action in conformity therewith[5] on a particular occasion, except:

    (1) **Character of accused.**[6] In a criminal case, evidence of a pertinent trait of character[7] offered[8] by an accused,[9] or by the prosecution to rebut the

---

Drafting Deficiencies

1. This title does more than just describe what the rule is about; it announces that the rule will generally prohibit character evidence to prove conduct. That's not necessarily bad, just inconsistent with other titles.

2. Technically, the *a* makes this read *Evidence of a person's . . . a trait of character*. No good. Drop the second *a*.

3. An unnecessary prepositional phrase. Make it *character trait*. More substantively, what is the practical difference between "character" and "character trait"? Could a witness simply testify that someone is a bad man, without more? The restyled rule keeps both ideas, but should it?

4. *For the purpose of* is a multiword preposition. Make it *to prove*.

5. Legalese.

6. An unnecessary prepositional phrase? *Accused's Character* is probably not very speakable. But far more often than not, a possessive is better than an *of*-phrase.

7. Again, make it *character trait*. Also, recall that (a) refers to both "character" and "trait of character." Why both items there, but only the latter here?

8. A passive-voice verb, and none of the exceptions to preferring the active voice seem to apply here. To make it active — *the defendant may offer* — we need to restructure paragraphs (1), (2), and (3) into complete sentences.

9. Converting to the active voice eliminates *by an accused*. Another prepositional phrase bites the dust.

same,[10] or if evidence of a trait of character[11] of the
alleged victim of the crime[12] is offered[13] by an accused
and admitted under Rule 404(a)(2),[14] evidence of the
same trait of character[15] of the accused offered by the
prosecution;[16]

(2) Character of alleged victim.[17] In a criminal
case,[18] and subject to the limitations imposed by[19] Rule
412, evidence of a pertinent trait of character[20] of the

---

10. Legalese.
11. Once again, make it *character trait*. Also, paragraphs (1) and (2) use
    trait of character four times, and then *character trait* the fifth time.
    But after saying *character trait* once, why not shorten to *trait* in all
    the later uses? We understand that that means "character trait."
12. Make it *alleged crime victim*. And note the four *of*-phrases in the 15
    words beginning with *or* and ending with *crime*. Quite a feat.
13. Passive voice.
14. An unnecessary cross-reference that better organization would cure.
    The organization is seriously flawed. Here's why. Paragraph (1) pur-
    ports to be about the accused's character, but in the middle we get a
    long condition having to do with a crime victim's character. That's
    what paragraph (2) is about — the victim's character. Hence the rep-
    etition in (2) of *evidence of a . . . trait of character of the alleged victim
    of the crime offered by an accused*. The restyled rule fixes the back-
    and-forth by creating three discrete categories in (2)(A), (B), and (C):
    the defendant's offering the defendant's own trait, and the prosecu-
    tor's responding; the defendant's offering the victim's trait, and the
    prosecutor's responding; and the prosecutor's offering the victim's
    trait of peacefulness in special circumstances.
15. See note 11.
16. For the record, paragraph (1) uses 15 prepositional phrases. The com-
    parable, repetition-free parts of the restyled rule — believe it or not
    — use 3.
17. Don't change this heading to a possessive unless you also change the
    heading for paragraph (1). Parallelism rules.
18. *In a criminal case* also appears at the beginning of paragraph (1). The
    restyled rule uses the phrase once — a sign of better organization.
19. Change *imposed by* to *in*.
20. See note 11.

alleged victim of the crime offered by an accused,[21] or
by the prosecution to rebut the same,[22] or evidence of
a character trait of peacefulness of the alleged victim[23]
offered[24] by the prosecution in a homicide case to rebut
evidence that the alleged[25] victim was the first aggressor;

> **(3) Character of witness.**[26] Evidence of the char-
> acter of a witness,[27] as provided in Rules 607, 608, and
> 609.[28]

The restyled rule improves on the current rule in three
basic ways. First, it restructures the rule. We now have
certain exceptions in a criminal case and exceptions for a witness. And the exceptions in a criminal case are broken down
into three categories. Second, those categories are set out in a
list that reads smoothly with the introductory language and
uses strong parallel constructions. Third, the restyled rule
dispenses with the slew of passive-voice verbs and prepositional phrases that bedevil the current rule.

---

21. As pointed out in note 14, almost all the words beginning with *evidence* are repeated from paragraph (1). So we get another passive-
voice verb and another blast of prepositional phrases.
22. Legalese.
23. Make it *the alleged victim's trait of peacefulness.*
24. Passive voice. The *be*-verb is implied: *evidence . . . [that is] offered.*
25. No need to repeat *alleged.*
26. See note 17.
27. One more time — make it *a witness's character.*
28. This paragraph, like (1) and (2), doesn't read well with the introductory language in (a): *Evidence of a person's . . . trait of character is not
admissible . . . except: . . . Evidence of the character of a witness, as
provided in Rules 607, 608, and 609.* The three paragraphs are technically items in a list (using the hybrid format mentioned earlier), but
the list is ill-formed.

Restyled Rule 404(a)
Character Evidence; Crimes or Other Acts
[later modified slightly, before final approval]

(a) Character Evidence.

> **(1) Prohibited Uses.** Evidence of a person's character or character trait is not admissible to prove that on a particular occasion the person acted in accordance with the character or trait.
>
> **(2) Exceptions in a Criminal Case.** The following exceptions apply in a criminal case:
>
> > **(A)** a defendant may offer evidence of the defendant's pertinent trait, and if the evidence is admitted, the prosecutor may offer evidence to rebut it;
> >
> > **(B)** subject to the limitations in Rule 412, a defendant may offer evidence of an alleged crime victim's pertinent trait, and if the evidence is admitted, the prosecutor may:
> >
> > > **(i)** offer evidence to rebut it; and
> > >
> > > **(ii)** offer evidence of the defendant's same trait; and
> >
> > **(C)** in a homicide case, the prosecutor may offer evidence of the alleged victim's trait of peacefulness to rebut evidence that the victim was the first aggressor.
>
> **(3) Exceptions for a Witness.** Evidence of a witness's character may be admitted under Rules 607, 608, and 609.

Old Rule 404(a)	Restyled Rule 404(a)
Character Evidence Not Admissible to Prove Conduct; Exceptions; Other Crimes	**Character Evidence; Crimes or Other Acts** [modified slightly before final approval]
(a) **Character evidence generally.** Evidence of a person's character or a trait of character is not admissible for the purpose of proving action in conformity therewith on a particular occasion, except:	(a) **Character Evidence.**
	(1) **Prohibited Uses.** Evidence of a person's character or character trait is not admissible to prove that on a particular occasion the person acted in accordance with the character or trait.
(1) **Character of accused.** In a criminal case, evidence of a pertinent trait of character offered by an accused, or by the prosecution to rebut the same, or if evidence of a trait of character of the alleged victim of the crime is offered by an accused and admitted under Rule 404(a)(2), evidence of the same trait of character of the accused offered by the prosecution;	(2) **Exceptions in a Criminal Case.** The following exceptions apply in a criminal case:
	(A) a defendant may offer evidence of the defendant's pertinent trait, and if the evidence is admitted, the prosecutor may offer evidence to rebut it;
(2) **Character of alleged victim.** In a criminal case, and subject to the limitations imposed by Rule 412, evidence of a pertinent trait of character of the alleged victim of the crime offered by an accused, or by the prosecution to rebut the same,	(B) subject to the limitations in Rule 412, a defendant may offer evidence of an alleged crime

or evidence of a character trait of peacefulness of the alleged victim offered by the prosecution in a homicide case to rebut evidence that the alleged victim was the first aggressor;

(3) Character of witness. Evidence of the character of a witness, as provided in Rules 607, 608, and 609.

victim's pertinent trait, and if the evidence is admitted, the prosecutor may:

(i) offer evidence to rebut it; and

(ii) offer evidence of the defendant's same trait; and

(C) in a homicide case, the prosecutor may offer evidence of the alleged victim's trait of peacefulness to rebut evidence that the victim was the first aggressor.

(3) Exceptions for a Witness. Evidence of a witness's character may be admitted under Rules 607, 608, and 609.

Symposium on the Restyled Federal Rules of Evidence: My Comments

This is from a symposium sponsored by the Willliam and Mary Law Review *and published in Volume 53, beginning at 1435 (2012).*

Well, there is so much to say and so little time. Actually, I've had my say on the restylings in some articles, one published in *The Scribes Journal of Legal Writing*, an article on the civil rules called *Lessons in Drafting from the New Federal Rules of Civil Procedure*.[1] It has scores of side-by-side examples. And I've written on the evidence restylings in a series of four articles in the *Michigan Bar Journal*.[2]

I trust that you can see the more obvious improvements in the rules, but there are countless less obvious improvements sentence by sentence. I'll give you just a couple of examples.

What is probably the worst small-scale fault in the old rules and, in fact, in all of legal writing? Unnecessary prepositional phrases. That's *unnecessary* prepositional phrases, not each and every preposition. Here's Rule 610, with the prepositions italicized:

> Evidence *of* the beliefs or opinions *of* a witness *on* matters *of* religion is not admissible *for* the purpose *of* showing that *by* reason *of* their nature the witness' credibility is impaired or enhanced.

There are either six or eight prepositional phrases, depending on how you count *for the purpose of* and *by reason*

---

[1]   *See* this book at 35.
[2]   *See* this book at 97, 105, 113, 119.

of, which are technically multiword prepositions or complex prepositions.

All right, so there are six or eight in old Rule 610. There is one prepositional phrase in revised Rule 610:

> Evidence *of* a witness's religious beliefs or opinions is not admissible to attack or support the witness's credibility.

Here's an example from Rule 612, about a witness's using a writing to refresh memory. When that happens, an adverse party is entitled to have the writing produced at a hearing (among other things). Then comes this piece:

> If it is claimed that the writing contains matters not related to the subject matter of the testimony the court shall examine the writing in camera, excise any portions not so related, and order delivery of the remainder to the party entitled thereto. Any portion withheld . . . . If a writing is not produced or delivered pursuant to order under this rule, the court shall . . . .

If it is claimed. By whom? Quick. If it is claimed by the producing party or the adverse party? You don't know. You have to wait and find out. Should have used the active voice. All right: *If it is claimed that the writing contains matters not related to the subject matter of the testimony.* Where's the comma after *testimony*? It's not optional. Then *the court shall examine the writing in camera, excise any portions not so related, and order delivery of the remainder to the party entitled thereto.* Note the inflated language and legalese: *excise*, *not so related* instead of *unrelated*, *remainder* instead of *rest*, and the musty *thereto*.

Next sentence: *Any portion withheld.* Withheld by whom? The producing party or the judge? It's actually the judge, but you don't know because the old rule switched from *excise* to *withheld*. If it had said *any portion excised* — which wasn't the best word to begin with — *any portion excised over objections*, then it would have been immediately clear that it was the judge.

Next sentence: *If a writing is not produced or delivered pursuant to order.* In other words, as ordered. Right? Not *pursuant to order.* Now, what does *pursuant to order* modify? Does it modify all the way back to *produced*? It's not supposed to. It really modifies only *delivered*, so the way to fix that is to start over again with *delivered*. One word does it: *If a writing is not produced or is not delivered pursuant to order.* And the *under this rule* after *order* is completely unnecessary.

You might just compare the clarity and flow of those three sentences with comparable parts of restyled Rule 612(b) and (c).

> **(b) Adverse Party's Options: Deleting Unrelated Matter.** [Adverse party's options set out. Then . . .] If the producing party claims that the writing includes unrelated matter, the court must examine the writing in camera, delete any unrelated portion, and order that the rest be delivered to the adverse party. Any portion deleted over objection must be preserved for the record.
>
> **(c) Failure to Produce or Deliver.** If a writing is not produced or is not delivered as ordered, the court may . . . .

The old rule had no headings, by the way. And it had 124 words total, as opposed to 90 in the new rule.

These are the fixes that we tried to make sentence by sentence, throughout the rules. We could continue this exercise for hours, but we won't. In the *Michigan Bar Journal* articles, I identified dozens of drafting deficiencies in the old rules in each of those four examples. You can't imagine unless you look closely: verbosity, unwieldy sentences, clumps of unbroken text, uninformative headings, disorganization, miscues, clumsy phrasing, repetition, multiple negatives, inflated diction, hardcore legalese (*pursuant to*, *herein*, *thereon*), bad punctuation, and, of course, that great troublemaker, *shall*.[3] No one thing in the restyling made the difference; it was the cumulative effect of myriad smaller things.

Now, are the new rules perfect? Of course not. You can always go back and find things and keep improving. Revising is endless. For one thing, there are for various reasons some structural flaws in the restyled rules. Rule 502 has a freestanding undesignated paragraph before the first subdivision. Several rules, like 801(d)(2), have so-called dangling text — text that continues after a vertical list without starting a new subdivision. 803 and 902 have different numbering from the other rules — 803(6), for instance, instead of 803(a)(6) as in the other rules.

There were inevitable challenges. Take old Rule 803, the hearsay exceptions. It starts out like a list: *The following are not excluded by the rule against hearsay*. But then you get what looks like a subdivision with a heading, 803(1) **Present Sense Impression.** There's a difference between a list and a subdivision, and 803 is really a hybrid. Then the items in the subdivisions, all those items in 803, that long list of 20-some exceptions — they're all sentence fragments. And some of those sentence fragments are very long, like 803(6), which is 108 words. But this was impossible to fix without starting over.

Naturally, my original drafts were modified as the process went along. Some of the calls I agreed with; some I didn't. Some were fairly easy, but many were hard, close calls. No doubt you'll hear about some of those today. For each one, there were principled arguments both ways. If the Advisory Committee voted that the call was substantive, that prevailed. If not, the style version prevailed, although

---

[3]   *See* this book at 87 (noting that the Words and Phrases online database cites more than 1,775 appellate cases interpreting *shall*); *see also* Bryan A. Garner, *Garner's Dictionary of Legal Usage* 952 (3d ed. 2011) (describing eight shades of meaning for *shall*).

the Committee would occasionally vote on a "sense of the Committee" regarding a style call. And so it went, for about three years.

During the civil-rules project, some people, mostly academics, objected that you can't do this. You can't do this successfully. You're bound to make substantive changes. Well, so far, through three restylings since 1998, the Advisory Committees have had to fix three, maybe four, inadvertent substantive changes — significant substantive changes. And if others come up, I'm sure they'll be fixed. But even if, down the road, there are ten times as many rules that need fixing, I'd say the restylings were still worth it. Why? Because of the state of the old rules.

Even apart from the gains in clarity and readability, we uncovered, through all the restylings, so many ambiguities, inconsistencies, gaps, and uncertainties — one after another — and we fixed most of them. Rule 806, to take just one example, had a critical ambiguity in shifting between *hearsay statement* and *statement*.[4] Here's the lesson: style affects substance. Good style improves the substance — always.

And then beyond that, even, is the matter of professionalism. Generations of law students — you — have had to wrestle with the old rules, not just the evidence rules but in all your code courses. It's a shame, and it's attributable in large measure to the way lawyers have forever drafted. Even as you struggle with these codes, you start to think that all this must be good practice. The trouble is that law schools have traditionally failed to teach legal drafting, which is a professional skill like any other, and a fundamental one, and one that needs to be learned. Most lawyers, no matter how brilliant, have not been trained in drafting. That's why the Standing Committee, going back to Robert Keeton and Charles Alan Wright and continuing since then, deserves immense credit for its commitment to a good, informed,

---

[4]   *See* this book at 115 nn.9 & 15.

consistent drafting style. And all four Advisory Committees, including the Evidence Committee, deserve immense credit for delivering on that commitment.

As I said at the end of the *Scribes Journal* article, the new rules will be far easier for law students to learn and for lawyers and judges to use. Besides that, the rules mark a long stride forward for professional competence in legal drafting.

Littering with Legalese, or Get a Load of This Release

Here's a short story.

In April 2007, the Center for Ethics, Service, and Professionalism at WMU–Cooley Law School sent an e-mail to the faculty and staff inviting us to participate in a Lansing "Clean Sweep." Participating organizations would pick up litter from their assigned area, a few city blocks, on a certain day. And Lansing would, at least for a while, be a brighter and tidier place.

I later learned that the event was being sponsored by a local bank. I admire the bank for undertaking the event. The people involved deserve credit and thanks for their community spirit. And the invitation struck a nerve with me. Like you, probably, I'm disgusted that people throw their trash out the car window or on the street for someone else to pick up. I'm even compulsive enough to pick up paper, plastic bottles, cans, and whatnot as I'm running. So, sure, sign me up.

Cooley's organizer said I would have to sign a release. Fine. She would drop it off at my office. Fine. She dropped it off at my office. Not fine.

The release was typical — and typically revolting. Once again, the public channels were polluted by legalese. Once again, readers — those who bothered to even try — were subjected to a form of writing that has been criticized and ridiculed for centuries. Once again, many of them must have been confused about what they were agreeing to. And once again, a few of them may have wondered whether legal documents have to be like this — and if not, why lawyers can't mend their ways.

133

Anyway, I e-mailed Cooley's organizer about who had written the release. She named the bank. "Is there a problem with legalese?" she asked. (The school's staff loves to hear from me on matters like this.) I said, "Yes, the legalese is silly and unnecessary." I suggested that she tell the bank's lawyers. Not that I thought it would do any good, but at least I'd have registered a protest.

She sent an e-mail and even followed up with a second one that said this: "Several weeks back I sent an e-mail at the suggestion of Professor Joe Kimble suggesting that you may want to have [the bank's] general counsel review the waiver you are using for the Clean Sweep project because he had some concerns about the legalese. I was just wondering if anyone had reviewed the wording and if any changes were made."

The response: "We would like to know about the concerns regarding legalese. We did solicit some outside help both from the city's legal staff and from a local firm." The response invited Cooley's organizer to participate in the next planning meeting. And I have since volunteered to rewrite the release.

The response was encouraging because legal departments more often react with indifference toward legalese and disdain for plain language. Over the years, I've heard from many nonlawyers who were trying to improve a form or letter or rule of some kind. After translating it into plainer language, they had to send it to the legal department. And the legal department told them that it wasn't legal. Usually, they received little or no explanation. The legal department just didn't like it; it didn't feel right. When there was an explanation, it usually had something to do with accuracy and precision — that old false criticism of plain language.[1]

Now I must ask you to wade through the Clean Sweep release and then consider some questions. Here it is.

---

[1]   *See* Joseph Kimble, *The Great Myth That Plain Language Is Not Precise*, in *Lifting the Fog of Legalese: Essays on Plain Language* 37 (2006).

CAPITAL CITY CLEAN SWEEP EVENT
WAIVER AND RELEASE FORM

IN CONSIDERATION of being permitted to participate in the Capital City Clean Sweep event, I (collectively, the undersigned participant and his/her parent or legal guardian), INTENDING TO BE LEGALLY BOUND, do hereby, for myself, my heirs, executors, administrators and representatives, ASSUME ALL RISK INHERENT IN MY PARTICIPATION, and further agree to, and do hereby release, waive, discharge, covenant not to sue and indemnify the City of Lansing, the Undersigned's Employer, or any Sponsoring Organization, or any of the officers, employees, sponsors, volunteers, representatives and agents of the City of Lansing, the Undersigned's Employer, or any Sponsoring Organization, of and from any claim in law or equity for injury or damages of any type whatsoever which I or he or they may make or incur arising out of my participation in the aforementioned activity, including payment of legal fees or costs incurred by the City of Lansing, the Undersigned's Employer, and any Sponsoring Organization, in defending against any such claim.

In addition, I authorize and grant permission to the City of Lansing staff to secure emergency medical and/or hospital treatment for myself as a participant in the Capital City Clean Sweep event.

I AM FULLY AWARE OF ALL THE INHERENT RISKS ASSOCIATED WITH MY PARTICIPATION AND DO HEREBY ASSUME AND ACCEPT ALL SUCH RISKS. I AM NOT AWARE OF ANY CONDITION, PHYSICAL OR OTHERWISE, WHICH COULD BE AGGRAVATED, WORSENED OR OTHERWISE ADVERSELY AFFECTED BY MY PARTICIPATION IN THE CAPITAL CITY CLEAN SWEEP EVENT.

I am signing this Waiver and Release form of my own free will and volition and I acknowledge that I have read this Waiver and Release Form and fully understand it.

_____   _____
Printed Participant Name   Date of Birth

_____   _____
Signature of Participant   Date

_____   _____
Participant's Address   City   Zip Code

_____
Name of Participant's Parent or Legal Guardian

_____
Signature of Participant's Parent or Legal Guardian

_____
Parent or Legal Guardian's Address   City   Zip Code   Phone No.

I realize that old forms are convenient and that lawyers are pressed for time. But how long would it take to make this release better? In a moment, I'll invite you to try. Before you do, though, consider these questions:

- Does the first sentence (a paragraph, actually) have to be 160 words?

- Is the recital of consideration necessary? If consideration is lacking, will the recital save the release? And isn't it obvious that the consideration here, if any, comes from being "permitted" to volunteer?[2]

- Is there any pattern or logic to the all-caps text? Is the capitalized language any more important than the uncapitalized *I . . . release*, for instance? And all-caps are notoriously hard to read in the first place.

- Why is ASSUME ALL RISK stated twice?

- Is it necessary to assume the risks in addition to releasing any claim?[3]

- A release can give up a claim only for ordinary negligence, not for gross negligence or worse.[4] Should the release reflect that limitation?

---

[2] *See* Kenneth A. Adams, *A Manual of Style for Contract Drafting* §§ 2.157, .160 (3d ed. 2013) ("[T]he traditional recital of consideration will, in most contracts, be ineffective to remedy a lack of consideration . . . . [O]n those rare occasions when it's not otherwise readily apparent whether a contract is supported by consideration, don't rely on a traditional recital of consideration. Instead, ensure that the recitals contain meaningful information pertaining to consideration.").

[3] *See Skotak v. Vic Tanny Int'l, Inc.*, 513 N.W.2d 428, 430 (Mich. Ct. App. 1994) (using language about "accept[ing] full responsibility" but not about assuming risks); *Dombrowski v. City of Omer*, 502 N.W.2d 707, 708 (Mich. Ct. App. 1993) (upholding a release that said nothing about assuming risks).

[4] *Universal Gym Equip. v. Vic Tanny Int'l, Inc.*, 526 N.W.2d 5, 6–7 (Mich. Ct. App. 1994).

- Is there a way to avoid repeating *the City of Lansing, the Undersigned's Employer, or any Sponsoring Organization?*
- Do you need this entire string: *release, waive, discharge, covenant not to sue and indemnify?* Doesn't *release* cover everything except indemnifying? A release *is* a discharge. And since a release completely extinguishes an underlying claim, there seems to be no point to adding a "mere" covenant not to sue.[5] Finally, note that *agree to . . . covenant not to sue* is gibberish. So is *waive . . . the City of Lansing . . . from any claim.*
- Do you need this entire string: *officers, employees, sponsors, volunteers, representatives and agents? Sponsoring Organization* was covered just a few words ago. What does *sponsors* add? What does *representatives* add?
- If the signer is indemnifying for claims by third parties, is that clear? How does the one word *indemnify* relate to the last part of the long sentence — beginning with *including* — about paying for legal fees? The signer is paying for having to defend *against any such claim.* Claim by whom? The signer? A third party? Who's suing whom?
- In that same part beginning with *including*, isn't the syntax garbled? Does it work to say that the signer is releasing the city and others from any claim, including payment of their legal fees? How do you release from payment of legal fees? This is the kind of trouble that a 160-word sentence causes.

---

[5] *J & J Farmer Leasing, Inc. v. Citizens Ins. Co. of Am.*, 696 N.W.2d 681, 684 (Mich. 2005) ("A release immediately discharges an existing claim or right. In contrast, a covenant not to sue is merely an agreement not to sue on an existing claim. It does not extinguish a claim or cause of action.").

- After the needless intensifier *whatsoever*, who is *he*? And who are *they*?
- In *the aforementioned* (ugh) *activity*, why has the earlier word *event* been changed to *activity*?
- What's with all the doublets and triplets: *I . . . do . . . and further agree to . . . and do hereby*; *of and from any claim*; *make or incur*; *authorize and grant permission*; *aggravated, worsened or otherwise adversely affected*; *my own free will and volition*?
- In the second paragraph, if *secure emergency medical and/or hospital treatment* were changed to *secure emergency medical or hospital treatment*, would anyone argue that you couldn't secure both?[6] (And I'd delete *or hospital*; it's covered by *medical . . . treatment*.)

Let's have a contest. I'll send a free copy of *Lifting the Fog of Legalese: Essays on Plain Language* to the first person who sends me an A revision of the release. Feel free to briefly annotate or footnote your draft if you'd like to explain a few points. E-mail it to kimblej@cooley.edu before February 25. I'll try to print the winning entry in next month's [Plain Language] column.

Maybe we can broom away some legalese from Michigan releases.

---

6   *See* Joseph Kimble, *To the Trashcan with* And/Or, Mich. B.J., Mar. 2007, at 44.

Cleaning Up a Release

Last month's column [February 2008] examined a typical release — one that volunteers were asked to sign before participating in a Lansing "Clean Sweep" event. I laid out my criticisms in that column and won't repeat them here. (One rant is enough.) I also offered a free copy of *Lifting the Fog of Legalese: Essays on Plain Language* to the first person to send me an A revision of the release. Below is the entry that I judged to be best, followed by my own revision.

Revision by Greg Schuetz, at Chrysler LLC:

CAPITAL CITY CLEAN SWEEP
<u>PARTICIPANT RELEASE AND MEDICAL AUTHORIZATION</u>

I wish to participate in the Capital City Clean Sweep. In return:

- I release the City of Lansing, my employer, and all Clean Sweep sponsors from any claim that their negligence injured or damaged me during the Clean Sweep.
- I agree to indemnify the City of Lansing, my employer, and all Clean Sweep sponsors against any claim that my negligence during the Clean Sweep injured or damaged a third party. I also agree to pay the legal fees and costs they incur in defending against any such claim.

If I am injured during the Clean Sweep, I give the City of Lansing permission to secure emergency medical treatment for me.

I am aware of the inherent risks of participating in the Clean Sweep and accept them. I am not aware of any physical or mental condition that would prevent me from, or could be aggravated by, participating in the Clean Sweep.

I have read this Release, understand it, and sign it voluntarily.

[SIGNATURE BLOCK]

My revision:

Release of Legal Claims

What I'm giving up

If I suffer any injury or damages from participating in the Capital City "Clean Sweep," I release, or give up, any legal claim that I might have against the following for their negligent conduct:

- The City of Lansing.
- My employer.
- A sponsoring organization.
- Any of their officers, employees, agents, or volunteers.

This release is binding on my legal representatives or anyone who tries to claim through me.

[*If the sponsor really wants an indemnity provision, which seems rather unreasonable . . .*

What I'm agreeing to pay for

If anyone listed above (in the four bullet points) is sued or has to pay anyone else because of my conduct, I will reimburse them for their legal costs, fees, and payments.]

My health; permission to get medical help

I don't know of any health condition of mine that could get worse if I participate in the Clean Sweep. I authorize the City of Lansing's staff to get emergency medical treatment for me during the Clean Sweep.

My understanding of this release

I have read this release, I understand it, and I sign it freely.

If the participant is not 18 years old—

Name (please print)	Name of Parent or Legal Guardian (please print)
Signature	Signature of Parent or Legal Guardian
Address	Date
City and Zip Code	
Date	

Wrong — Again — About Plain Language

In a way, you have to admire someone who has spent decades campaigning against plain language — unsuccessfully — and who still carries on. As Jack Stark acknowledges in a new foray,[1] "many statutory drafters have accepted the school and use its precepts." Maybe that's because the school and its precepts have something important to offer — even to respected veteran drafters like Mr. Stark.

What's troubling is to see the recirculation of criticisms that are demonstrably false and that have been answered so many times. You have to wonder: how could anyone who knows the plain-language literature keep trotting out these inaccuracies and arguments? It's hard to figure.

At any rate, before I take on each of these mischaracterizations of plain language, I'll go right to the make-it-or-break-it point.

The charge: plain language generates errors.

Mr. Stark anchors his criticism on a before-and-after example from an Internet plain-language site. He rattles off a series of pronouncements about changed meaning, asserts that "the proof is in the pudding," and finds unpalatable "a method of drafting that generates so many errors."

---

[1] *Plain Language*, The Legislative Lawyer, http://www.ncsl.org/legislators -staff/legislative-staff/research-editorial-legal-and-committee-staff/june -2012-plain-language.aspx.

Let's set aside the multitude of successful plain-language projects around the world[2] and the endless stream of examples that advocates have put forward for at least 50 years, beginning with David Mellinkoff.[3] Let's accept the questionable premise that one unsuccessful piece of plain drafting raises doubt about all the other ones. Let's look at this supposedly half-baked pudding.

It's Title 12, Section 602.16, of the U.S. Code of Federal Regulations. Here's the before and after:

> **Aggregating Requests.** A requester may not file multiple requests at the same time, each seeking portions of a document or documents, solely in order to avoid payment of fees. When the Farm Credit Administration reasonably believes that a requester, or a group of requesters acting in concert, is attempting to break a request down into a series of requests for the purpose of evading the assessment of fees, the Farm Credit Administration may aggregate any such requests and charge accordingly. One element to be considered in determining whether a belief would be reasonable is the time period over which the requests have occurred.

> **Combining Requests.** You may not avoid paying fees by filing multiple requests at the same time. When FCA reasonably believes that you, alone or with others, are breaking down a request into a series of requests to avoid fees, we will combine the requests and charge accordingly. We will assume that multiple requests within a 30-day period have been made to avoid fees.

First point: the revision was adopted in 1999, after publication and an opportunity for public comment. At the

---

[2] *See, e.g.*, Joseph Kimble, *Writing for Dollars, Writing to Please: The Case for Plain Language in Business, Government, and Law* 64–102 (2012).

[3] *The Language of the Law* (1963).

time, the agency said the new rule "amends FCA [Farm Credit Administration] regulations on the release of information under the Freedom of Information Act to [among other things] reflect new fees."[4] So lo and behold, it's quite possible that any changes from the previous version were intended. Or it's possible that any differences were considered insignificant in practice.

Now for the substance. And here we need to know the context. People must pay a per-page fee for requests, but they get the first 100 pages free. Hence section 602.16, designed to prevent people from avoiding fees by splitting up a single request into multiple requests for parts of a document or documents.

Here are Mr. Stark's assertions (in the first sentence of each bullet) and my responses (in the paragraph following):

- *"Aggregate*, which means 'add up,' has been changed to *combine*, which means 'blend together.'"

    But *combine* also means "to unite into a single number."[5] That's precisely what the drafters meant and how readers would understand that term in context.

- *"Seeking portions of a document or documents* has been eliminated; the rules now apply to any request."

    So is there a difference in practice? Mr. Stark doesn't explain. If, before, you sought part of a document, that was considered a request. And it still is.

- *"Solely* has been eliminated, allowing other causes such as forgetting that a request has already been made and that the agency erred."

---

[4]   64 Fed. Reg. 41, 770 (Aug. 2, 1999).

[5]   *Merriam–Webster's Collegiate Dictionary* 246 (11th ed. 2003).

Now, how likely is that? Does anybody forget a formal request under the Freedom of Information Act? And the original version applied to multiple requests "at the same time . . . solely . . . to avoid payment of fees." So previous requests didn't even figure into the original version. Mr. Stark's point here is elusive.

- *"Acting in concert* has been replaced by *with others*, which includes requests made at the same time by chance and requests with several names on them."

Acting at the same time by chance is not the same as acting "with" someone to avoid fees. And if a request has several names on it, the signers were presumably acting in concert, just as they were acting with others. In any event, the new wording won't cause the agency to reach a different conclusion than it would have under the old wording.

- *"Series* . . . has been replaced with *multiple* . . . ."

No, it hasn't. In both versions, the first sentence uses *multiple requests*, and the second sentence uses *a series of requests*. Then the revised third sentence uses *multiple requests* again, consistent with its use in the first sentence. Mr. Stark says that *multiple* means "many, not more than one." But in fact, it does also mean "consisting of . . . more than one."[6] This insistence on a single meaning for a word has now become a multiple error.

- *"Is attempting to break a request down* has been changed to *are breaking down a request."*

---

6   *Id.* at 816.

Again, what does it matter? The original version was not distinguishing between attempting to break down and actually breaking down; it was not creating an "attempted" violation, like attempted murder; it was not trying to identify an act that is separate from and occurs before actually breaking down a request. In short, the word *attempting* was superfluous in the original: it should have been *is breaking down a request* — exactly like the revised version. All the original did was open the door to a silly, unintended distinction.

- "*May aggregate* has been changed to *will combine*, which is a change from a permission to a requirement."

Right, the agency obviously decided, as a matter of policy, to take a stricter approach. But even then, the agency presumably retains some measure of discretion.

- Multiple requests within 30 days now give rise to "an automatic assumption, not merely a consideration," as in the original.

Once again, this change is so obvious that the agency drafters must have intended it. In fact, they changed from the indefinite *time period over which the requests have occurred* to *a 30-day period*. Mr. Stark calls this change "inexplicable." It's actually as clear as can be: the drafters wanted to be more specific.

All in all, then, the changes in meaning that Mr. Stark summons up are nonexistent, insignificant in practice, or deliberate. The revised version is not only shorter and clearer but also more accurate. *More* accurate, not less. And so it is that Mr. Stark's case against plain language comes unmoored.

Don't get me wrong: you can find mistakes and flaws in plain drafting. But anyone who enjoys that pursuit would have much more fun with old-style drafting, where ambiguities, inconsistencies, and uncertainties flourish in all the verbosity and disorder. I took four examples from the old Federal Rules of Evidence and pointed out 33, 31, 18, and 28 drafting deficiencies in those examples.[7] Finding a flaw in a plain-language statute or rule does not mean that plain language doesn't work or that we're stuck in reverse, with no choice but to draft in the arcane style so roundly criticized for centuries. An occasional mistake does not undo all the good and potential good.

The charge: plain language makes wrong assumptions and is "shot through with fallacies."

Now we turn to the rest of Mr. Stark's criticisms, almost all of which are delivered without any supporting authority. Below is a brief response to each one.

- Advocates of plain language assume that "laypeople frequently read statutes."

  Not exactly. We think that "Acts . . . (and regulations too) are consulted and used by a large number of people who are not lawyers."[8] And we think drafters should make statutes and regulations intelligible to the greatest possible number of intended readers, especially those

---

[7] *See* this book at 97, 105, 113, 119.
[8] New Zealand Law Comm'n, Report 104, *Presentation of New Zealand Statute Law* 14–15 (Oct. 2008), http://www.lawcom.govt.nz/our-projects /presentation-new-zealand-statute-law?id=885 (giving examples of people who "refer to legislation in their jobs" and other examples of when people may consult it in their personal lives).

who are directly affected.[9] Mr. Stark notes that people don't read the Internal Revenue Code. Of course not. It's a complete mess. (And it seems like an extreme example in any event.) But shouldn't people be able to read and understand — without travail — a regulation that tells them what the fee is for requesting information under the Freedom of Information Act (just to pick an example)? Who are laws for, after all? Only some clique of lawyers?

- Advocates assume that citizens "have a right to read simplistic statutes."

Our view is not that simplistic. We do think citizens should have the greatest possible access to the law. Mr. Stark says that if one wants citizens to have that access, then provide "explanatory publications." That's fine; we recognize the value and versatility of citizens' guides.[10] But why shouldn't the law be as clear as possible to begin with? Why make this an either/or choice? Besides, the clearer we make the law, the less need there will be for any sort of guide.

- "Most of [the] advocates are not professional drafters but academics and others who may never have drafted a bill."

---

[9] Kimble, *Writing for Dollars, Writing to Please* at 31–33; *see also* Letter from the American Bar Ass'n, Sec. of Admin. Law & Reg. Prac., to Senators Joseph Lieberman and Susan Collins 2 & n.4 (Dec. 18, 2012), www.americanbar.org /content/dam/aba/administrative/administrative_law/s2337_plain _writing_act.authcheckdam.pdf ("strongly endors[ing]" plain language in regulations and expressing "real concern . . . with text that may be understandable, but only to an expert who expends real effort in mastering the text").

[10] *See* Law Reform Comm'n of Victoria, *Plain English and the Law* 57–58 (1987; repr. 1990) ("[Explanatory texts] are likely to reach a wider audience than the originals, and to be more widely used than other means of informing the public.").

Well, that would be news to legislative drafters in many countries — the UK, Ireland, New
Zealand, Australia, Canada, Sweden, the EU,
and others — who have endorsed plain language.[11] That would be news to the more than
1,750 members of the Commonwealth Association of Legislative Counsel — a group that
"has helped promote plainer drafting across
the world and share knowledge on how to go
about it."[12] Indeed, the 2007–2011 president of
CALC and former head of the legislative-
drafting offices in Hong Kong and Victoria,
Australia, offers this declaration: "We shouldn't
still be having to defend plain language in the
twenty-first century."[13]

• Advocates believe that "it is more important to
be clear . . . than to be accurate."

This charge could not be more wrong. I re-
sponded to Mr. Stark on this same point many
years ago.[14] No reputable advocate has ever said
that clarity trumps accuracy. Yes, I have said,
"Your main goal is to convey your ideas with the
greatest possible clarity."[15] But *of course* I mean
"convey your ideas accurately." Nobody who
knows my work — or the work of any other
advocate — could possibly think otherwise.
We all take the need for accuracy as blindingly

---

[11] *See* Office of the Scottish Parliamentary Counsel, *Plain Language and Legis-*
   lation 19–28 (2006), http://Scotland.gov.uk/Resource/Doc/93488/0022476
   .pdf.
[12] Kimble, *Writing for Dollars, Writing to Please* at 102.
[13] E-mail from Eamonn Moran to the author (Oct. 20, 2012).
[14] *Answering the Critics of Plain Language*, 5 Scribes J. Legal Writing 51,
   53–60 (1994–1995).
[15] Kimble, *Writing for Dollars, Writing to Please* at 5.

obvious.[16] But we do think that, with rare exceptions, clarity and accuracy are complementary — not competing — goals. As Reed Dickerson, the father of modern-day legal drafting, wryly put it: "The price of clarity, of course, is that the clearer the document the more obvious its substantive deficiencies."[17] Or in the words of another expert: "The purposes of legislation are most likely to be expressed and communicated successfully by the drafter who is ardently concerned to write clearly and to be intelligible."[18] Time after time, we have seen clarity improve accuracy by uncovering the ambiguities and errors that traditional drafting tends to hide. Yet if in some instance, on some point, accuracy and clarity really are at odds, then accuracy wins. It goes without saying — almost.

• "Typically, there are lists of 10 or 12 [plain-language] rules, far too few for an enterprise as difficult as statutory drafting."

First of all, they are guidelines, preferences, principles — not inflexible rules. And the complete list of guidelines numbers in the dozens.[19] Natu-

---

[16] *See, e.g.,* Michèle M. Asprey, *Plain Language for Lawyers* 92 (4th ed. 2010) ("We need to be accurate, precise *and* able to be understood by all our likely readers."); Robert D. Eagleson,*Writing in Plain English* 5 (1990; repr. 1994) ("Writers of plain English documents use language their audience can understand, and ensure that their documents are complete and accurate statements of their topics. They do not leave out important details . . . ."); Kimble, *Writing for Dollars, Writing to Please* at 40 ("Nobody doubts that legal writers need to aim for accuracy and the right measure of precision.").

[17] *Materials on Legal Drafting* 265 (1981) (quoting one of Dickerson's earlier articles, now difficult to access).

[18] G.C. Thornton, *Legislative Drafting* 52 (4th ed. 1996).

[19] *See* Kimble, *Writing for Dollars, Writing to Please* at 22 (citing authorities that list 42, 50, 40, 45, and 25 with lots of subpoints).

rally, you will find top-ten lists and the like, as advocates try to pull out a handy set of especially important principles. But we are not so unenlightened as to think that that's all there is to it. We have always taken an expansive view of plain language, sought to ground it in research,[20] been open to reexamination, and realized that "bare guidelines are not enough."[21]

- As an example of a rule that he says "makes no sense," Mr. Stark cites the rule "to address you" — that is, to address readers as *you*.

But here again, advocates do not insist on *you* in statutes. Rather, they recommend using *you* in consumer documents[22] — including regulations — whenever doing so works. Ask yourself: Does *you* seem to work in the regulation we reviewed earlier? Is there any doubt that *you* refers to the person who is requesting information? In the right context, *you* is a great aid to readability. It puts readers in the picture.[23]

- "[Another] fallacy is the command that short sentences should be used."

Nobody commands. We typically say to *prefer* short and medium-length sentences. Or we

---

[20] *See, e.g.,* Daniel B. Felker et al., *Guidelines for Document Designers* (American Institutes for Research 1981) (citing empirical research for each guideline); Karen Schriver & Frances Gordon, *Grounding Plain Language in Research*, Clarity No. 64, at 33 (Nov. 2010), http://www.clarity-international .net/clarity_journal/archives (describing the current state of research and recommending further efforts).

[21] Kimble, *Writing for Dollars, Writing to Please* at 5.

[22] *Id.* at 10.

[23] Rudolf Flesch, *How to Write Plain English: A Book for Lawyers and Consumers* 44–50 (1979); Janice C. Redish, *How to Write Regulations and Other Legal Documents in Clear English* 24 (1991).

say to break up long sentences (one of the oldest and worst curses of traditional drafting) or a pattern of long sentences. Long sentences are not usually needed to connect ideas. You can make connections in other ways.[24] You can use vertical lists. You can pull longish exceptions into new sentences. You can use patterns such as "The court may require . . . . Or the court may require . . . ." There are lots of ways. It's telling that Mr. Stark doesn't give examples of long sentences that cannot be broken up. And by the way, look again at the revised regulation. Original: 27, 51, and 23 words (= 34 on average). Revised: 14, 31, and 17 words (= 21 on average).

- Mr. Stark criticizes my example of *give, devise, and bequeath* as redundant in a will. He says that "*give* denotes making a gift from one live person to another."

  But certainly not in a will. The giver is gone. The giver is giving by this instrument, the will. Bryan Garner quotes "the leading American scholars on the law of wills" to "resolve any doubt" about not needing a triplet.[25] They state: "'I give' will effectively transfer any kind of property, and no fly-specking lawyer can ever fault you for using the wrong verb."[26] I invite anyone to find a published case to the contrary.

- "The most damaging Plain Language rule is to write only words that are commonly used by laypeople in ordinary speaking and writing."

---

[24] *See* this book at 44–48.
[25] *Garner's Dictionary of Legal Usage* 391 (3d ed. 2011).
[26] Jesse Dukeminier Jr. & Stanley M. Johanson, *Family Wealth Transactions* 11 (1972).

Another straw man. You may extract from some sources a guideline like "Use simple words," but the explanation that follows will usually make clear that this is not a rigid prescription. A fair reading of the plain-language literature does not support any "rule" to write "only" ordinary words.[27]

- "Some legal terms have no Plain Language synonyms."

We know. And we have never said otherwise. But we have said — and shown — that (1) terms of art are a small part of most legal documents,[28] (2) terms of art should be explained in consumer documents,[29] and (3) many terms that lawyers might think of as untranslatable can in fact be replaced with ordinary words.[30]

- "I would be embarrassed to admit that my job is to write dumbed down statutes."

---

[27] *See, e.g.*, Asprey, *Plain Language for Lawyers* at 232 (providing a side-by-side list of plain and more formal expressions, but noting that the formal one is "perfectly fine in some circumstances"); Joseph Kimble, *Plain Words*, in *Lifting the Fog of Legalese: Essays on Plain Language* 164 (2006) ("By all means, use the longer, less familiar word if you think it's more precise or accurate."); Richard C. Wydick, *Plain English for Lawyers* 58 (5th ed. 2005) ("If an unfamiliar word is fresh and fits your need better than any other, use it — but don't *utilize* it.").

[28] Kimble, *Writing for Dollars, Writing to Please* at 36.

[29] *Id.; see also* Christopher R. Trudeau, *The Public Speaks: An Empirical Study of Legal Communication*, 14 Scribes J. Legal Writing 121, 149–50 (2011–2012) (confirming the public's overwhelming preference that legal terms be explained in an attorney's communication).

[30] *See, e.g., Law Words: 30 Essays on Legal Words & Phrases* (Centre for Plain Legal Language 1995), http://www.clarity-international.net/documents/law_words.pdf (containing short essays on 28 terms like *joint and several* and *right, title and interest*).

Ah, yes, the old dumbing-down argument — another one that should have been buried long ago.[31] It's not dumbing down to write clearly for your reader in legal, government, and business documents. It takes great skill, and readers love it. Try to find a reader who protests that a legal document is too clear, that he or she is insulted by the clarity, that the writer should have used a more traditional, legalistic, dense, verbose, contorted style. In fact, no fewer than 25 studies show that readers of all kinds — judges, lawyers, clients, consumers — strongly prefer plain language to the old style, understand it better and faster, are more likely to comply with it, and are much more likely to read it in the first place.[32]

There's no need to go on answering critics. Plain language is changing the landscape — as witness the new Federal Rules of Civil Procedure and Federal Rules of Evidence. And I'd dare to say that in the minds of most writers and drafters, the intellectual debate is over.

---

[31] Kimble, *Writing for Dollars, Writing to Please* at 11–14.
[32] *Id.* at 134–66.

PART TWO

On Legal Writing Generally

You Think Anybody Likes Legalese?

I was an early convert to plain language — or plain English as it was called then — when it began to make headway in the 1970s. From the start, I was convinced that plain language is a just cause: right in its strong criticisms of traditional legal style, right in its call for reform, and right in its general prescriptions. Of course, my understanding of it has evolved and broadened over the years, but it remains for me a passion — a life's work. And the work will need to go on long after I've gone on. A reformer, someone once told me, needs a geologist's sense of time.

I started teaching legal writing at WMU–Cooley Law School as an adjunct in 1982, and that turned into a full-time position in 1984. Naturally, I brought with me a commitment to teaching a clear and plain style. Those first years are still vivid — the classrooms, students' names, even who sat where. Like any other teacher, I remember the hits and misses, the good moves and the blunders, and the intensity of it all. (Almost from the start, I used live grading: I read a student's paper and graded it with the student sitting next to me.) I especially remember a couple of early challenges to my spiel and instructions on plain writing.

Two of the Many Myths About Plain Language

One night a student waltzed into class with a tray of food. At the break after the first hour, I caught his attention and privately reminded him about the school's policy against food in the classroom. Maybe that put him in the mood to take issue. At any rate, during the next hour, he raised his hand and asserted: "A client wants to see you driving a

Cadillac, not a little Honda. [This was 1984.] Why wouldn't
he want to see you using big, impressive words?" I said
something about the questionable analogy between size and
value in cars, on the one hand, and words, on the other. I said
that trying to keep people dumb about the emptiness of legalese does us no credit and will eventually lead to disrespect.
And I must have said — I hope I said — something about
writing to communicate. But that question was telling —
as a version of the common myth that plain words are pedestrian, dull, uninspiring; they are beneath the dignity of
professional writers.

This myth, like a vampire, will probably never die, although I tried again to bury it in part 2 of my book *Writing
for Dollars, Writing to Please*. It will continue to spook inse-
cure writers, drain strength from their prose, and fill it with
pretension. And the myth will not easily give way to reason
and argument and evidence because it preys on a vague, un-
developed sense of literary quality.

But another myth will — or should — yield to evidence
in the form of hard numbers. And that brings me to the second challenge that students raised in those early years of my
teaching plain writing.

Too many times to ignore, I heard different versions of
essentially the same question: how do we know that plain
language is acceptable in the real world outside law school?
What do judges say? What's the attitude among lawyers? Will
I please or displease my readers? Maybe plain language is too
newfangled for comfort. How do we know? Of course, I had
no good answer — so a student and I decided to conduct a
survey of Michigan judges and lawyers.

This was 30 years ago, in 1987, and I've since reported on
the survey many times.[1] No need to do it again here, except
to say that given six pairs of passages from different legal
documents — one written in plain language and the other

---

[1]   *See* Joseph Kimble, *Strike Three for Legalese*, in *Lifting the Fog of Legalese:
    Essays on Plain Language* 3 (2006).

in traditional style — 425 Michigan judges and lawyers preferred the plain versions by margins running from 80% to 85%. And the same survey was repeated in three other states, with strikingly similar results.

What I haven't mentioned until now is my high anxiety while waiting for the results. As I remember, we gave the judges and lawyers about a month to respond. My student colleague was collecting the results, and I didn't ask for updates. I had no idea what to expect. (O ye of little faith.) What if my students — some of them, anyway — were right to be dubious or at least uncertain? Maybe traditional style is so entrenched that most legal readers won't see it as inferior. But they did. It was one happy, affirming day when I got the news.

That study was published the same year as another study (which I didn't know about at the time) testing legalese versus plain English in appellate briefs. Guess which style was rated "substantively weaker and less persuasive" and led readers to infer that the writers who used it came from less prestigious firms?[2]

I'm deliberately avoiding detail because I don't want you to dwell on those early studies alone. I'd like you to appreciate the full weight of the evidence against legalese. And for that, you need to see the complete picture.

What the Evidence Shows

In part 5 of *Writing for Dollars, Writing to Please*, I cite and summarize 50 studies of business, government, and legal documents. Of the 50, no fewer than 18 involved legal documents. And the documents were of all kinds: statutes, administrative regulations, judicial opinions, briefs and

---

[2] Robert W. Benson & Joan B. Kessler, *Legalese v. Plain English: An Empirical Study of Persuasion and Credibility in Appellate Brief Writing*, 20 Loyola L.A. L. Rev. 301, 301 (1987).

other lawsuit papers (complaints, motions), jury instructions, court forms, class-action notices, contracts, and client
letters. The readers, too, were of all kinds: judges, lawyers,
administrators, clients, and other members of the public.
So the evidence could hardly be more complete — or more
compelling.

Do you think anybody likes legalese? No. Nobody. Or
I should say no body — not judges or lawyers or the public
at large. All those groups strongly prefer plain language and
find it more effective and persuasive. Besides that, they understand it better and faster, perform more accurately when
they have to deal with it, and are more likely to read it in the
first place. Please, purveyors and defenders of legalese, just
look at the studies of your readers.

Now, I can hear the objections. "But clients expect legalese." If they do, we should be ashamed of having conditioned
them to expect it because they certainly don't like it. "But
my boss likes it the old way." Then either try gentle persuasion or wincingly do what your boss wants, bide your time
until you can decide, and know that your boss's attitude and
style are retrograde. "But most lawyers are still churning out
legalese." That's the great disconnect: they forget as writers
what they prefer as readers. (Not to mention the sheer force
of habit and inertia.) "But plain language isn't accurate, isn't
precise — isn't safe." The biggest myth of all — the Goliath
myth. I've flung a few stones at it before, arguing that plain
language is actually *more* precise than traditional style.[3]

The case for plain language is altogether solid. All the
myths and misconceptions about it have been debunked.
What remains is for lawyers to summon the will and develop
the skill to do it. Their readers have spoken.

---

[3] *See* Joseph Kimble, *Writing for Dollars, Writing to Please: The Case for
Plain Language in Business, Government, and Law* 37–43 (2012); *The
Great Myth That Plain Language Is Not Precise*, in *Lifting the Fog of Legalese* at 37; *Wrong — Again — About Plain Language*, this book at 141.

Tips for Better Writing in Law Reviews (and Other Journals)

I originally prepared these tips with help from my colleagues in the Research & Writing Department at WMU–Cooley Law School. For years, we read dozens of student notes submitted for the Scribes Law-Review Award. And each year, we saw many of the same distractions and deficiencies. So I tried to put together an antidote. The tips are now being distributed by Scribes to all U.S. law reviews.

Structural and Analytical Tips

- Write a compelling introduction, one that's sure to grab the reader. Avoid platitudes ("torture is inconsistent with American values") and banal generalities ("the limits of *Roe v. Wade* are still being tested in federal courts"). State your claim, your main thesis, in a forceful way. Or use a concrete example to illustrate the issue, and then state your claim. For good examples, see *Academic Legal Writing*, by Eugene Volokh, and *Scholarly Writing for Law Students*, by Elizabeth Fajans and Mary Falk.

- Avoid the sleep-inducing, but ubiquitous, front-end description of what you're going to cover in each part. Your headings should provide the guidance that readers need.

- Back up your analysis with accepted jurisprudence, current law, or some other accepted theory from another discipline. But be selective and pick the most important authorities; do not feel the need to survey the entire history of law on the subject. Save that for your book.

- Be painstakingly accurate in representing what the authorities say; otherwise, your reader will distrust everything else in your article.

- Raise and address counterarguments as you go, in their logical places. Don't save them all for a separate part at the end.

- Generally avoid long paragraphs — those longer than six sentences (and not six long ones). Try to average three or four sentences. Another guideline: average no more than 150 words.

- Use topic sentences. Make sure that each one connects with the point you were just making and summarizes the point you're about to make in the new paragraph.

Footnoting and Formatting Tips

- Minimize talking (substantive) footnotes. Save footnotes for citations and, when appropriate, short parentheticals. Here's a good test: if you think the material is worthy of a footnote, try to weave it into the text; if you can't, then it probably won't be very useful to your reader as a footnote either. Remember: a page with a longer footnote section than text is a bad sign. Page after page in that mode is a nightmare.

- Put almost all footnote numbers at the end of the textual sentences, not midsentence.

- Again, for most propositions, cite just one or two authorities (and possibly a contrary authority). Occasionally, you might cite more to show the sheer weight of authority on an important or controversial point.

- Don't feel obligated to footnote every sentence. A series of *Id*.s is often overkill. Use some judgment and give the reader some credit. If, for example, you're summarizing a court's reasoning in a few sentences within the same paragraph and the court's reasoning appears on consecutive pages, one citation should do. An adroit writer who cares about avoiding footnote clutter can signal the consolidation to the reader ("the court distinguished *Jones* in two ways").

- Guide the reader with plenty of informative headings and subheadings. Not informative: "The Majority View." Informative: "The Majority View: *Shall* in Rule 56 Does Not Mean *Must*."

- Don't use ALL CAPITALS or <u>underlining</u> for headings. Use gradations of **boldface**, or **boldface** combined with ***italicized boldface***.

- Use graphic devices such as bullet dots, numbered lists, charts, and diagrams to make your points easy to grasp.

Stylistic Tips

- Above all, make the text lively and readable. Avoid clichés like the plague. Try in places for fresh, evocative prose.

- Write in a style that's conversational but polished. Two good models: *The Green Bag* and *The Scribes Journal of Legal Writing*.

- Write your article so that any literate person can understand it. Too often, authors write law-review articles while thinking only about their academic colleagues. But the more useful and effective articles are those that are easily understood by academics, judges, lawyers, students, and laypeople alike.

- Vary sentence length, but generally write crisp short and medium-length sentences; aim for an average sentence length of 20 to 25 words.

- Use connectors to create flow in your document. And allow yourself to start sentences with *And, But,* and *So*; in fact, prefer those conjunctions to their equivalents.

- Minimize long block quotations. And weave quotes deftly into your substantive point. Avoid leading into quotations with unhelpful set phrases like *The court stated* and *The statute provides in pertinent part.*

- Avoid string citations, or use parentheticals telling the reader why you have cited multiple sources.

- Don't turn verbs into nouns. Use *consider,* not *give consideration to; concluded,* not *came to the conclusion.* Examples like these abound.

- Root out unnecessary prepositional phrases. Not *the duty of the landlord,* but *the landlord's duty;* not *an order of the court,* but *a court order.*

- Avoid a slew of initialisms. It's ridiculous to convert *the Martin Luther King Scholarships* to *MLKS.* After the first full mention, find a convenient shorthand: *King Scholarships.* If an initialism is already in the common vocabulary, fine; use it. There's no need to convert *IRS* to *the Service,* or to write *The Internal Revenue Service (IRS)* on the first mention, as if your reader needed to be told what the short form will be.

- Hyphenate phrasal (compound) adjectives like *small-business owner* and *civil-rights law.*

- Embrace the dash. Shun the slash.
- Allow yourself to use *I* if that comes naturally in the sentence.
- Avoid inflated diction like *prior to* and *during the course of*.
- Avoid lawyerisms like *pursuant to* and *inter alia*.
- Don't use a longer, unfamiliar word when a shorter, more familiar one will do. Know the plain equivalents of inflated words and phrases, and prefer them in almost all instances. Use plain English!
- After you have prepared your first draft, cut it by at least 10% — ideally, more.
- Check and then double-check spelling and punctuation.

Reference and Reading Tips

- Build a reference library. At the least, you should have and habitually consult these books by Bryan Garner: *Garner's Modern English Usage*, *Garner's Dictionary of Legal Usage*, and *The Redbook*.
- Commit to a serious reading program, if you haven't already. Among the possible starting points: Richard Wydick, *Plain English for Lawyers*; Bryan Garner, *The Elements of Legal Style*; Joseph Kimble, *Lifting the Fog of Legalese* (with additional recommended books in Appendix 2); Joseph Williams & Joseph Bizup, *Style: Lessons in Clarity and Grace*; John Trimble, *Writing with Style*.
- In everything you read, be a keen observer. Notice what good writers do. Jot down words, phrases, techniques. Make it a lifelong ambition to learn more about writing and to keep improving.

How to Dominate Your Reader — and Make Stewie Griffin Proud

This is a talk I gave to law students at the 2013 National Conference of Law Reviews, for the annual Scribes dinner. The dinner honors the winner of the Scribes Law-Review Award, given to the year's best student-written note or comment.

When it comes to legal writing, most lawyers seem to have a contrarian attitude. They flout accepted principles of good writing. They cling to habits and practices that have been criticized, not to say ridiculed, for centuries. And they continue to think this style is effective, impressive, perfectly comprehensible, and necessary for legal precision — contrary to what the rest of the world says and contrary to the strong evidence presented by reformers within our own profession.

But let's not daydream about reform. To help shield you from change, I'm offering some solid advice for succeeding in this contrarian, backward-looking world of legal writing generally and law-review writing in particular. Unfortunately, your article will never win the Scribes Law-Review Award, but so what? You don't want to stand out or be different. So here's how to mark yourself as a traditional, establishment legal writer and editor — and no mere purveyor of simple, direct, uncluttered prose.

I've got 12 extra-special tips for staying the familiar course — and showing reformers what they can do with all this plain-language poppycock.

1. Try to have more than half of every page devoted to footnotes. More footnotes than text. After all, readers care about what you're saying, but they care

more about whether you've cited and annotated every authority even remotely on point since the beginning of recorded history. And the digressions in footnotes serve nicely to break up the tedium of your line of thought. Legal readers expect to have two trains running. That's just how we do it. We're sophisticated about these things.

2. Of course, you must — without exception — footnote every sentence, even if you produce a long series of *Id.*s or even if the point is a matter of common knowledge. If you say — and by the way, I note this with pain, since they swept the Detroit Tigers — if you say, "In 2012, the San Francisco Giants won the World Series," you must footnote it. And you should probably add in a parenthetical that the World Series is played for the North American championship of the game of baseball.

3. A related secret. Practice the art of the midsentence footnote. The current record is 9 footnotes in a 21-word sentence. Midsentence footnotes are a sign of how really meaty your sentence is. And the reader benefits because the constant looking up and down is good exercise for the eye muscles and even the neck.

4. Use as many prepositional phrases as possible. Readers appreciate this kind of wordiness. Too brisk a pace can be very tiring. So never write "the landlord's duty to maintain the common areas" when you can write "the duty *of* the landlord *with regard to* the maintenance *of* the so-called common areas." You know, add some speed bumps — for the reader's own good.

5. Use *pursuant to* as often as possible. Some people say that it reeks of legalese, but we know better. It adds little grace notes to your writing. We love the

poetry, the musicality, of purSOOant TO. So forget about the common, pedestrian word *under*. Not *under Rule 10*, but *pursuant to the provisions of Rule 10*. And while you're at it, never use *before* or *after* when you can write *prior to* or *subsequent to*. We all know that Robert Frost made a rare misstep when he wrote, "But I have promises to keep/And miles to go before I sleep." It should have been: "And miles to go prior to my sleeping." Same with "'Twas the night prior to Christmas." In short, strive for inflated, high-flown, bookish language. Never mind what George Bernard Shaw said: "In literature, the ambition of a novice is to acquire the literary language; the struggle of the adept is to get rid of it." What does he know?

6. Strive for an average sentence length of about 35 words. Anything less will not challenge your reader enough. Short sentences are for wimps. And you'll open your writing to charges of being unsophisticated, dumbed down, babyish, base, dull, and drab. As your model, look to Tom Wolfe or Norman Mailer. Of course, they're virtuosos, but we might be too. So practice concocting elaborate, intricate sentences like theirs. You can do it!

7. Likewise, test your readers' mental agility by saving the main verb — the main action — for late in the sentence. It creates a nice sense of dramatic anticipation about what's happening. For example: "The employees, who had tried — no, attempted — for years to resolve their grievance through a series of meetings with company representatives and an arbitrator, finally SUED in federal court." Wait a minute. A simple verb like *sued* isn't good enough. Make it *brought suit*. Better yet: *instituted litigation*.

8. Never start a sentence with *But*. We all know that "How-ev-er," with a comma, is more rhythmic and stately. Pay no attention to how you talk or what good writers do. Lincoln slipped when he wrote, "But in a larger sense, we cannot dedicate, we cannot consecrate, we cannot hallow this ground." We learned from our high-school teachers that it's incorrect to start a sentence with *And*, *But*, or *So*. We also learned that we should never split an infinitive, never end a sentence with a preposition, never use the first person, and never use a contraction. Heaven forbid that you should write "i-t-apostrophe-s." We have standards to uphold, and superstitions to believe in.

9. Never use a dash. The reason is simple: dashes are way too informal for the lofty enterprise of a law-review article. Besides, then you'll never have to worry about the difference between a hyphen and a dash, or between an en-dash and an em-dash. The world would be a better place if we could just whack a few of those pesky punctuation marks.

10. Create as many initialisms or acronyms as possible. The more, the merrier. Take a name like "The Society to Preserve the Blues." For later references, don't shorten it to "The Society" or "The Blues Society." Make it "SPB." Besides all the pages you'll save, when you use "SPB" on page 3 and then again a few pages later, the reader will probably have to thumb back through to remember what it stands for — thus re-viewing your article (although in reverse). That's quite a nice payoff to you for annoying the reader just a little.

11. Pay no attention to navigational aids or to formatting. Readers are thrilled to be faced with long stretches of uninterrupted text, without any head-

ings or subheadings to point the way. And do not stoop to using bullets or diagrams or graphics of any kind. That kind of namby-pamby stuff is for kids only. Also, make sure to use tight line spacing, narrow margins, and lots of all-caps and underlining. Stick with typewriter tools.

12. Don't try for anything humorous or light. Ignore Fred Rodell's complaint — he was a Yale law professor — that "it seems to be a cardinal principle of law-review writing and editing that nothing may be said forcefully and nothing may be said amusingly." It's just too risky to try for anything fresh or expressive, or to use an occasional allusion or metaphor. Readers are more comfortable with clichés, such as: "Legal writing is like the weather: everybody complains about it, but nobody does anything about it." And remember: when you use an expression like this, you should try hard to track down the source. If all else fails, attribute it to Mark Twain. He's always a good bet.

If you do all these things, you'll be well on your way to accomplishing several notable goals:

- You'll confound all the writing experts — you'll prove them so wrong about good writing. You did it your way, the old way.

- As I suggested earlier, you'll put yourself squarely within the venerable [cough] tradition of scholarly legal writing. You'll be sharing the attitudes and practices of many — I daresay most — legal writers.

- You'll mark yourself as erudite, learned, soon to be a juris doctor. You've earned the right to show off a little.

- You'll give your prose style a weight and complexity that matches your deep thinking. Here again, all the great intellects and stylists who say that even complex ideas can be expressed clearly — they just can't be right. Complex ideas require dense prose. Anyway, it's too much trouble to be clear. Takes too much practice and skill and reading.

- You'll counter the growing trend toward plain legal writing — and prove that all the myths about plain language weren't really myths after all. It just doesn't work. Legalese is tried and true. It never causes trouble.

- Finally, you'll force your reader to spend extra time reading your article, extra time absorbing your thoughts. In the words of the Beatles — my generation — you know that can't be bad. You'll achieve reader domination. Then you can echo Stewie Griffin — your generation, gotta love him — "Victory is mine!" Of course, Stewie is sometimes a little delusional, isn't he?

Further law prof sayeth naught.

A Study in Editing

This article about improving law reviews appeared in Volume 11 of
The Scribes Journal of Legal Writing. *Since it touches on editing, I
asked the author whether, in Volume 12, we could show the edits I
made, and he graciously agreed. The changes are in boldface; only
the punctuation might be a little hard to see.*

I remember the horror as if it were yesterday. Yet it was September 1994, on the train from New Haven to New York
City. I had just received the edited manuscript of my first
article accepted by a U.S. law review. I opened it expecting
to feel a warm inner glow of accomplishment. **Instead,** ~~D~~dis-
appointment flooded me, followed by a rising anger. The
editors had rewritten much of it~~;~~ to "improve the readability
and clarity of expression." It was perhaps a tad easier to read.
It was also wildly inaccurate. The topic was documentary-
credit law~~.~~ — ~~An~~ **an** intricate and arcane field full of fine
distinctions~~;~~**,** which the editors had trampled underfoot in
their quest for clarity.

    I had to revise the manuscript extensively to restore its
accuracy. This creature to which I had given birth, lovingly,
over ~~twelve~~ **12** months~~;~~ had been butchered**,** and now I had
to stitch it back together.[‡] (Today**,** I would give the editors
the choice of limiting themselves to essential **substantive**
amendments ~~of substance,~~ or ~~of~~ returning the piece. As a
junior academic**,** I did not have, or did not feel I had, ~~this
choice~~ **that power**.)

[‡] Today I would give the editors the choice of limiting themselves to essential
  amendments of substance, or of returning the piece. As a junior academic I
  did not have, or did not feel I had, this choice. [Moved to text.]

The cause of the butchery was simple. Most law-review editors in the U.S. system do not know how to edit~~,~~ and, in many cases, do not fully understand what they are editing.

Most U.S. law-review editors are second- and third-year law students. They are typically highly intelligent and highly driven. Serving on law review is a role that falls to the best students and, although very time-consuming, is usually accepted by them as a prestigious marker of achievement ~~within law school~~.

These student editors decide which articles to publish, typically without the benefit of ~~referee's~~ **referees'** reports. As students, they have little to base their selection of articles ~~up~~on, and one suspects that the status of the **author's** school ~~with which the author is affiliated~~ may count heavily.

The editors usually edit the articles extensively**,** seeking to improve ~~their~~ **the** written expression, and **they** check ~~each and~~ every citation for substantive and formal accuracy. ~~Each function is of questionable importance, and is~~ **Both functions are** questionably performed.

Editing for Readability

On the issue of editing for style and readability, two examples will suffice.

One of my sentences read, "The global economy has changed profoundly in the past 30 years." The editors recast it as, "Over the past 30 years, the global economy has changed dramatically." The test for editing should be whether the change ~~is essential~~ **improves clarity**, not **whether it suits the editors'** personal taste.

In another instance, I had written of a "non-remunerated" reserve requirement. The editors suggested "unremunerated." Either way, no one gets paid, so does it matter?

In all, the editors made 405 changes to my manuscript of some 19,000 words of text. Fifteen of these changes, by my assessment, improved readability or clarity and were worth making. ~~Three hundred and ninety~~ **The other 390** changes added nothing substantial. Of these, 81 had to be reversed because the editors had distorted the meaning. This article was on a topic beyond most law students' knowledge. Excluding the small number of changes to the footnotes, the editors on average made one change for every 50 words. They changed every third sentence of the article — a massive waste of their time and energy, and mine.

I don't mean to question the value of good editing. Not in the least. All writers — even the best — can benefit from good editing. I just wonder how much student editing is good.

~~Citation Checking~~ Checking Citations

The other preoccupation of student editors of ~~US~~ **U.S.** law reviews is checking citations. This is a curious practice ~~as~~ **because** it seems based on the premise that law professors are sloppy in their research or make things up.*

The list of sins that can plausibly be laid at the feet of law professors is conceivably quite long: laziness, insecurity, egotism, competitiveness, obsessiveness about details, and a tendency to be self-indulgent loners, not team players. Catch any law ~~teacher~~ **professor** on a bad day and ask ~~them~~ about the flaws of ~~their~~ colleagues, and you may get a longer list. But you almost certainly won't be told, even on a very bad day, that ~~their~~ **those** colleagues are sloppy or make up sources. The idea is plain silly. We have almost no incentive, financial or otherwise, to be sloppy or ~~overly creative~~ **overcreative** and every incentive to be careful, ~~as~~ **because** our professional reputation rides on it.

---

* Editors' note: But professors do make mistakes in providing names and numbers, and a self-respecting law journal aims for a consistent citation form.

Yet my research assistant last week assembled copies of 28 sources for one of my manuscripts, so that we can mail them to the student editors of a leading ~~US~~ U.S. law review who have been unable to locate them. She couldn't find every source in my office — perhaps for some I worked straight from the books, **or** perhaps they have been mislaid. But each was before me when I wrote the article.

~~But~~ **A law professor's** mere assertions of accuracy ~~by a law professor~~, **though,** are insufficient to dampen the zeal of student editors. This morning they have told me that the references to the sources I cannot produce will be deleted and replaced with sources that they will find. Good luck, folks! If you cannot find sources ~~on~~ about international finance law with accurate citations when your law school is in Manhattan, good luck with finding your own.

What a ~~massive~~ waste of time and intellectual effort.

~~Peer Review, a Potential Solution~~ A Potential Solution: Peer Review

One solution would be to move to a peer-review process for law reviews in the U.S. This is the most common system in Australia and the ~~United Kingdom.~~ **U.K.** Law journals are typically edited by scholars. Law students are often involved, but the editorial decisions are made by faculty members, sometimes in conjunction with students, but based on reports from referees.[1]

---

[1] For an interesting and robust analysis of the state of play of law journals in Australia, ~~see~~ **compare** John Gava, *Law Reviews: Good for Judges, Bad for Law Schools?* 26 Melb. U. L. Rev. 560 (2002) **(generally condemning law reviews, presumably even those that are peer-reviewed),** with Michael Kirby, *Foreword: Welcome to Law Reviews*, 26 Melb. U. L. Rev. 1, 4 (2002) **(generally defending the value of law reviews, especially those that are peer-reviewed — as an "increasing number" are in Australia);** for a ~~consideration~~ **view** of ~~their~~ **the** situation in Canada, see Kathryn Feldman, *Remarks About the Value of Student-Run Law Journals*, 17 Windsor

The faculty editors weed out unsuitable or unpublishable articles. Surviving submissions are then sent to one~~,~~ referee (or more commonly two~~, referees~~). It is a blind refereeing process: the referees do not know the author's identity ~~of the author~~ or ~~their~~ institutional affiliation. And ~~T~~this is taken quite seriously ~~—~~ . ~~b~~Beyond removing the author's name and institution from the cover page, considerable care is usually ~~brought to bear~~ taken to ensure that nothing in the text or footnotes suggests the author's identity. Referees are selected for their specialist expertise in the manuscript's subject ~~of the manuscript~~ and are routinely sought beyond the institution with which the journal is affiliated, and often abroad.

The process ~~is often~~ can be slow~~,~~ because referees are often slow to respond. This is a weakness~~.,~~ ~~B~~but it is fair. It ~~does not~~ neither advantages eminent scholars or those from leading law schools nor disadvantages young scholars or those from less prestigious schools.

The editing is also largely limited to content. In my experience, referees' reports usually suggest some changes to the argument and occasionally identify a few infelicities of style. In stark contrast, the comments ~~of the~~ by student editors of ~~US~~ U.S. law reviews tend to focus almost exclusively on form, not substance. And their editing usually does not, in my experience, improve the writing. [Perhaps we should have said "too often does not improve the writing."]

~~Both factors~~ These tendencies are to be expected.

Content is what matters. No sane person reads law reviews for the limpid clarity of the ~~written expression~~ writing or the illumination ~~on offer from~~ offered by the footnotes. Content is what matters, and content is what expert referees' reports focus ~~up~~on.

Rev. Legal & Soc. Issues 1 (2004). [Converted to *ALWD Citation Manual* form; almost all the details were correct. The same goes for the footnotes that follow.]

Yet when one is unqualified to assess or comment ~~upon~~ the content of a piece, all ~~that is~~ that's left to do is to ~~critique~~ **inexpertly change** its written expression and **agonize over its** references.

Interestingly, law journals in Australia and the U.K. tend to prefer shorter articles over longer ones~~,~~ — 6,000 to 10,000 words is considered ~~an~~ ideal ~~length,~~ — and do not share the obsession of their U.S. cousins with abundant footnotes. Sophisticated arguments can be readily developed in under 10,000 words, and longer articles, in my view, often communicate less effectively.

~~I am~~ **I'm** tempted to speculate that the excessive length and footnote density of most ~~US~~ **U.S.** law-review articles ~~is a~~ **are** products of the feelings of safety engendered in student editors by long and heavily referenced pieces. After all, such pieces offer the illusion of substance~~,~~ and thus appear to be safe bets for editors with little or no expertise in the ~~field the subject of the article~~ **article's subject**. Perhaps ~~they~~ **these pieces** offer the same illusion to their authors, ~~particularly~~ **especially** those seeking tenure at their faculties~~, which may well be the other reason for their proliferation~~.[2]

In any event, the height of footnote absurdity in the U.S. is illustrated by one of my articles that was accepted subject to my adding another 40 footnotes to it. The editors were troubled **that** it had only 30. I was older by now, and refused, but said the student editors were welcome to add some if they wished, and they did. All 40 extra references!

A move to peer review would definitely improve the quality of U.S. law-review articles. It would also, I ~~contend~~ **believe,** tend to counter the love of length **that** these journals exhibit. Size is all well and good, in its place, but ~~clear communication is~~ **it** rarely ~~promoted by it~~ **promotes clear communication.** An expert is qualified to assess the worth of an argument~~,~~ and **will** not substitute length and **the** number

---

[2]   James C. Raymond, *Editing Law Reviews: Some Practical Suggestions and a Moderately Revolutionary Proposal*, 12 Pepp. L. Rev. 371, 375–77 (1985).

of footnotes as measures of quality. An expert would also typically object to having to read a 25,000-word piece.

Admittedly, ~~A~~ a move to peer review is **unlikely** today ~~unlikely~~ in most U.S. law schools. ~~The effort of serving~~ **Some faculty members may serve** as editors **of journals** ~~and referees would prove a burden on law faculty members and, remember, laziness was listed earlier as one of their credible character failings~~, **but I suspect that far fewer would be willing to serve as referees.**

Serving as a journal editor is a tremendous amount of work**,** but **it at least** confers ~~considerable~~ status and exposes one to the latest writing in one's field, ~~particularly~~ **especially** if it is a specialist journal.

Refereeing**, on the other hand,** is just plain hard work. Legal scholars in Australia, the U.K., and elsewhere undertake it out of a sense of obligation and a belief **that** ~~it is~~ **it's** an essential part of our shared scholarly enterprise. ~~But a tendency to being self-indulgent loners and not team players was identified as another credible law professor failing.~~ We outside ~~America may be no less lazy or self-indulgent (although we are certainly less pampered) than our American brethren but we~~ **the U.S.** are used to doing this unpaid work, and we accept it as essential quality control for journals. We also typically think that writing ~~referee's~~ **referees'** reports is important scholarly work. **So** ~~Our resumes would~~ **our résumés** usually reflect prominently any journal~~s of which~~ **that** we are the editor **of**~~, and would mention the journals~~ **or** that regularly invite**s** us to serve as **a** referee~~s~~.

In short, serving as editors of journals and as referees is part of our scholarly culture~~;~~ — and cultures can be slow and difficult to change.

Conclusion

The solution to "the editors don't know how to edit" part of the problem is conceptually simple — teach them. ~~If one would~~ **You might** expect this to be fairly obvious to ~~universities~~ **law schools,** ~~one would be wrong~~ **but apparently it's not**. While the lamentations ~~regarding~~ **about** student-edited law reviews are legion,[3] very few law schools **formally** teach their student editors ~~formally~~ how to do their job.[4]

~~It is~~ **It's** true that editing is a subtle task requiring considerable judgment and ~~it~~ is therefore difficult to teach. ~~However, it is~~ **But it's** equally true that it can be broken down into sequential steps and taught~~;~~.[5] ~~a~~**A**nd training ~~in editing~~ would **at least** improve an editor's efforts.

~~And t~~**T**raining ~~in how to edit~~ would not, ~~of course~~ **though,** address the other part of the problem: that student ~~law review~~ editors are not qualified to choose between potential articles by assessing their substantive quality. It is difficult to see anything short of peer review **as** properly addressing this problem, so the challenge is how to shift U.S. law-faculty culture so that **faculty members willingly bear**

---

[3] *See* Richard A. Epstein, *Faculty-Edited Law Journals*, 70 Chi.-Kent L. Rev. 87 (1994); The Executive Board of the Chicago-Kent Law Review, *The Symposium Format as a Solution to Problems Inherent in Student-Edited Law Journals*, 70 Chi.-Kent L. Rev. 141 (1994); Wendy J. Gordon, *Counter-Manifesto: Student-Edited Reviews and the Intellectual Properties of Scholarship*, 61 U. Chi. L. Rev. 541 (1994); James Lindgren, *An Author's Manifesto*, 61 U. Chi. L. Rev. 527 (1994); Alan W. Mewett, *Reviewing the Law Reviews*, 8 J. Legal Educ. 188 (1955); Richard A. Posner, *Against the Law Reviews: Welcome to a World Where Inexperienced Editors Make Articles About the Wrong Topics Worse*, Legal Affairs 57 (Nov.–Dec. 2004); Richard A. Posner, *The Future of the Student-Edited Law Review*, 47 Stan. L. Rev. 1131 (1995).

[4] James Lindgren, *Student Editing: Using Education to Move Beyond Struggle*, 70 Chi.-Kent L. Rev. 95, 98 (1994) **(encouraging "increased faculty help, oversight, and training" that includes "editing seminars for student editors").**

[5] Anne Enquist, *Substantive Editing Versus Technical Editing: How Law Review Editors Do Their Job*, 30 Stetson L. Rev. 451 (2000).

the burdens of a peer-review system ~~are borne willingly by faculty members~~.

The answer may well be leadership, by a leading journal. ~~It is~~ **It's** unlikely to come from the journals ranked one, two, ~~or~~ **and** three in the nation, ~~as~~ **because** they will probably feel they have more to lose than gain from change. ~~However, it~~ **But leadership** may well come from journals ~~ranked perhaps between four and ten~~ **that rank a bit lower** and want~~ing~~ to ascend the ladder.

All it would take is **for** one ~~of~~ **or** two highly regarded journals to provide the lead. If one or two such journals were to announce **that** they were now faculty-edited and **that** credible submissions would be peer-reviewed, and **if** this ~~was~~ **were** to lead to a rise in the rankings, then others would likely follow. For the first-movers, finding potential referees ~~should~~ **might** be ~~quite easy~~ **easier than you would think,** ~~as~~ **since** the prestige of serving as a referee for a highly ranked journal should hold some appeal ~~(remember insecurity)~~, **and** the novelty of being asked ~~will~~ **would** count for much~~, and law professors are perhaps less lazy than this piece has intimated~~.

If these cutting-edge journals were to go a step further and announce that the preferred ~~length of~~ manuscripts **length** was between 6,000 and 10,000 words, this would provide even further impetus to their ascension. Does anyone really want to write 30,000 words on an incredibly narrow topic~~, i.e.;~~ **that is,** does anyone enjoy writing tenure pieces? Surely a safer and more enjoyable road to tenure is four or five 10,000-word articles rather than two articles of 30,000 and 20,000 words ~~respectively?~~. The traditional route is a stressful one — it makes a lot ride on two articles, especially when some articles, ~~especially~~ early in one's career, just don't seem to want to come together~~, for whatever reason. Certainly t~~**The** evidence is that as scholars become more senior, their articles become shorter and their footnotes fewer.[6] **So** ~~These~~ **those** cutting-edge journals would, presumably, have considerable appeal to more senior scholars.

The worlds of legal practice, law schools, and law reviews are intensely competitive. ~~it is~~ **It's** time for some good law reviews to become great ones by harnessing this competition to improve their quality~~,~~ and to ~~thereby~~ lead U.S. law reviews into the peer-reviewed world ~~which is~~ **that's** the norm in law outside the U.S. — and the norm in most disciplines everywhere.

---

[6]   *See* Ira Mark Ellman, *A Comparison of Law Faculty Production in Leading Law Reviews*, 33 J. Legal Educ. 681, 683 (1983).

Please Vote on Two Citation Formats

I'd like to try an experiment. It's not exactly scientific, but the results could be revealing — and useful.

There's a story behind the experiment, but I'll save the story for the July [2010 Plain Language] column. For now, I'll just encourage all you loyal readers to vote. Below are three pairs of examples. Only the second pair has slight differences; otherwise, they are identical except for the placement of the citations. The examples marked #1 do it one way; the examples marked #2 do it another. Which do you think reads better?

Please send me an e-mail (kimblej@cooley.edu) and say in the subject line "I vote for #1" or "I vote for #2." No split votes, please.

#1	#2
On February 10, 2009, Burton issued a memorandum to Plaintiff reassigning her from her bid position as a school officer to a general corrections officer at TCF. (Defs.' Ex. L.) Defendant Barnhardt testified that the move was not punitive, and that Plaintiff was not disciplined in any way. (Barnhardt Dep. at 113–14, Defs.' Ex. J.) Plaintiff receives the same pay, maintains the same rank, and works on the same shift. (*Id.* at 113.) However, her job assignments now rotate. (*Id.*) And, as set forth above, she no longer has a set schedule, with weekends and holidays off. (Pl.'s Dep. at 10, Pl.'s Ex. 153.) Plaintiff also testified that her previous position as a school officer was less dangerous, because it has less contact with the prison population. (*Id.* at 153–54.)	On February 10, 2009, Burton issued a memorandum to Plaintiff reassigning her from her bid position as a school officer to a general corrections officer at TCF.[1] Defendant Barnhardt testified that the move was not punitive, and that Plaintiff was not disciplined in any way.[2] Plaintiff receives the same pay, maintains the same rank, and works on the same shift.[3] However, her job assignments now rotate.[4] And, as set forth above, she no longer has a set schedule, with weekends and holidays off.[5] Plaintiff also testified that her previous position as a school officer was less dangerous, because it has less contact with the prison population.[6] ——————————— [1] Defs.' Ex. L. [2] Barnhardt Dep. at 113–14, Defs.' Ex. J. [3] *Id.* at 113. [4] *Id.* [5] Pl.'s Dep. at 10, Pl.'s Ex. 153. [6] *Id.* at 153–54.

#1	#2
Defendants assert that Plaintiff's alleged adverse action is too trivial to survive summary judgment. It is undisputed that Plaintiff's reassignment did not result in a loss of pay, a change of shift time, or a drop in rank. . . .	Defendants assert that Plaintiff's alleged adverse action is too trivial to survive summary judgment. It is undisputed that Plaintiff's reassignment did not result in a loss of pay, a change of shift time, or a drop in rank. . . .
Sixth Circuit case law does not support Defendants' position. Where the record demonstrates that "being transferred . . . causes Plaintiffs to suffer harm to their reputations . . . and can negatively impact their daily experiences including their commute, coworker friendships, and community relationships," *Leary v. Daeschner*, 349 F.3d 888, 901 (6th Cir. 2003), the Sixth Circuit has held that "involuntary transfer from one job to another is action that 'would likely chill a person of ordinary firmness from continuing to engage in that constitutionally protected activity.'" *Id. (quoting Bloch v. Ribar*, 156 F.3d 673, 679 (6th Cir. 1998) (impairment of reputation, humiliation, mental suffering subject to compensatory damages)). The Sixth Circuit has held that even when the employee suffers no loss in pay or rank, such a transfer can qualify as an adverse action for purposes of retaliation claims. *Id.; see also Boger v. Wayne County*, 950 F.2d 316, 321 (6th Cir. 1991) (where "extreme embarrassment, humiliation, extreme mental anguish, and loss of professional esteem" was alleged, "Plaintiff need not have suffered loss of salary, promotional opportunities, seniority or other monetary deprivations to have a cognizable interest protected by the First Amendment or the equal protection clause.").	Sixth Circuit case law does not support Defendants' position. A record may demonstrate that being transferred "causes Plaintiffs to suffer harm to their reputations . . . and . . . negatively impact[s] their daily experiences including their commute, coworker friendships, and community relationships."[1] If so, then the "involuntary transfer from one job to another is action that 'would likely chill a person of ordinary firmness from continuing to engage in that constitutionally protected activity.'"[2] The Sixth Circuit has held that even when the employee suffers no loss in pay or rank, such a transfer can qualify as an adverse action for purposes of retaliation claims.[3]
	──────
	[1] *Leary v. Daeschner*, 349 F.3d 888, 901 (6th Cir. 2003).
	[2] *Id.* (quoting *Bloch v. Ribar*, 156 F.3d 673, 679 (6th Cir. 1998) (impairment of reputation, humiliation, mental suffering subject to compensatory damages)).
	[3] *Id.; see also Boger v. Wayne County*, 950 F.2d 316, 321 (6th Cir. 1991) (where "extreme embarrassment, humiliation, extreme mental anguish, and loss of professional esteem" was alleged, "Plaintiff need not have suffered loss of salary, promotional opportunities, seniority or other monetary deprivations to have a cognizable interest protected by the First Amendment or the equal protection clause.").

#1	#2
Once Plaintiff meets her burden of establishing a prima facie case of retaliation, the burden shifts to the employer who "may 'show[] by a preponderance of the evidence that it would have reached the same decision . . . even in the absence of the protected conduct.'" *Rodgers v. Banks*, 344 F.3d 587, 602 (6th Cir. 2003) (quoting *Mt. Healthy City Sch. Dist. Bd. of Educ. v. Doyle*, 429 U.S. 274, 287 (1977)). This latter burden, however, "'involves a determination of fact' and ordinarily is 'reserved for a jury or the court in its fact-finding role.'" *Id.* (quoting *Perry v. McGinnis*, 209 F.3d 597, 604 n.4 (6th Cir. 2000)). Defendants argue they can meet this burden as a matter of law, asserting that they would have reassigned Plaintiff based on "complaints from staff and prisoners about the unnecessarily harsh manner in which she performed her duties as school officer." (Defs.' Br. at 16.)	Once Plaintiff meets her burden of establishing a prima facie case of retaliation, the burden shifts to the employer who "may 'show[ ] by a preponderance of the evidence that it would have reached the same decision . . . even in the absence of the protected conduct.'"[1] This latter burden, however, "'involves a determination of fact' and ordinarily is 'reserved for a jury or the court in its fact-finding role.'"[2] Defendants argue they can meet this burden as a matter of law, asserting that they would have reassigned Plaintiff based on "complaints from staff and prisoners about the unnecessarily harsh manner in which she performed her duties as school officer."[3] --- [1] *Rodgers v. Banks*, 344 F.3d 587, 602 (6th Cir. 2003) (quoting *Mt. Healthy City Sch. Dist. Bd. of Educ. v. Doyle*, 429 U.S. 274, 287 (1977)). [2] *Id.* (quoting *Perry v. McGinnis*, 209 F.3d 597, 604 n.4 (6th Cir. 2000)). [3] Defs.' Br. at 16.

Where Should the Citations Go?

In the May [2010 Plain Language] column, I asked readers to vote on two citation formats — one putting citations in the text, the other putting them in footnotes. I gave three pairs of side-by-side examples that were the same except for the placement of citations. The examples were clearly from the same source, and the second one referred to "Sixth Circuit case law" and to what "the Sixth Circuit has held." For convenience, here's the third example only:

#1	#2
Once Plaintiff meets her burden of establishing a prima facie case of retaliation, the burden shifts to the employer who "may 'show[] by a preponderance of the evidence that it would have reached the same decision . . . even in the absence of the protected conduct.'" *Rodgers v. Banks*, 344 F.3d 587, 602 (6th Cir. 2003) (quoting *Mt. Healthy City Sch. Dist. Bd. of Educ. v. Doyle*, 429 U.S. 274, 287 (1977)). This latter burden, however, "'involves a determination of fact' and ordinarily is 'reserved for a jury or the court in its fact-finding role.'" *Id.* (quoting *Perry v. McGinnis*, 209 F.3d 597, 604 n.4 (6th Cir. 2000)). Defendants argue they can meet this burden as a matter of law, asserting that they would have reassigned Plaintiff based on "complaints from staff and prisoners about the unnecessarily harsh manner in which she performed her duties as school officer." (Defs.' Br. at 16.)	Once Plaintiff meets her burden of establishing a prima facie case of retaliation, the burden shifts to the employer who "may 'show[] by a preponderance of the evidence that it would have reached the same decision . . . even in the absence of the protected conduct.'"[1] This latter burden, however, "'involves a determination of fact' and ordinarily is 'reserved for a jury or the court in its fact-finding role.'"[2] Defendants argue they can meet this burden as a matter of law, asserting that they would have reassigned Plaintiff based on "complaints from staff and prisoners about the unnecessarily harsh manner in which she performed her duties as school officer."[3]
	[1] *Rodgers v. Banks*, 344 F.3d 587, 602 (6th Cir. 2003) (quoting *Mt. Healthy City Sch. Dist. Bd. of Educ. v. Doyle*, 429 U.S. 274, 287 (1977)).
	[2] *Id.* (quoting *Perry v. McGinnis*, 209 F.3d 597, 604 n.4 (6th Cir. 2000)).
	[3] Defs.' Br. at 16.

I asked readers to vote for the example marked #1 or #2, posing the question, "Which do you think reads better?"

One important point before announcing the winner: this is not about whether to use so-called talking, or substantive, footnotes. It's not about whether to drop incidental points — those bits you just can't quite fit in — to the bottom of the page. I'm no fan of talking footnotes, and I don't use them in this column or in *The Scribes Journal of Legal Writing*. But that's another debate. The question before us is where to put the references, the bare citations (and any brief parentheticals). Should they go in the text or in footnotes?

All right, the polls are closed and the votes counted. Readers preferred format #2 — citations in footnotes — and by a fairly comfortable margin, 111 to 81. That's at least refreshing, if not remarkable, given our strong tradition of textual citations and the common complaint that the profession is notoriously slow to change. So good for us.

Although I did not ask voters to comment, quite a few did. It's interesting that people who voted for #1 tended to write somewhat more detailed comments. People who voted for #2 tended to make short comments like these:

- "Less cluttered and facilitates reading."
- "Much easier to read and understand."
- "#2 reads clearly without distraction."
- "Smoother flow when reading. More cohesive."
- "There's nothing to talk about. They [#2] read so much better."

As many of you may know, the most forceful proponent of footnoted citations is Bryan Garner, America's preeminent authority on legal language and writing. In his book *The Winning Brief*, he summarizes the pros and cons (the bracketed responses on the right are his; I added the boldface):

Footnoted Citations (Without Substantive Footnotes)[1]	
Pros	**Cons**
1. They shorten the average sentence length. 2. They make paragraphs more coherent and forceful. 3. They let readers focus on ideas, not numbers. 4. They eliminate the problems with string citations. 5. They expose poor writing and poor thinking in the text, thereby promoting clearer writing and thinking. 6. They result in fuller discussions of controlling caselaw. 7. They result in much greater efficiency in conveying ideas. 8. They make legal writing accessible to far more people.	1. Legal readers have already learned one system: textual citations. [**Yes, but legal writers have proved unable to handle the convention. . . . Besides, readers see citation-free text everywhere *except* in legal writing.**] 2. Citations often contain important information about precedents. [**All that important stuff should be woven into the prose anyway. Otherwise, readers accustomed to skipping over in-text citations are just as likely to miss your authority there as below.**] 3. Readers shouldn't have to glance at the bottom of the page. [**Right: brief-readers shouldn't ever have to read footnotes. All that's down there are volume numbers and page numbers — and optional parentheticals.**] 4. Writers can more easily fudge what authorities say. [**That's silly: too many fudge in the text right now.**] 5. The practice results in a confusion of literary genres: scholarship vs. practical writing. [**But the absence of substantive footnotes signals that this isn't scholarship.**] 6. You can't retrain yourself to read past superscripts. [**If you can retrain yourself to read past two lines of citational numbers, you can retrain yourself to read past a tiny superscript.**] 7. It requires more effort: you can't simply paste quotations and citations into your writing. [**If it results in greater accessibility for all readers, surely it's worth the effort.**]

[1] *The Winning Brief* 179 (3d ed. 2014).

In the next sentence after this chart, Garner observes: "Whereas the pros are hard to answer — often unanswerable — the cons are mostly easy to counter."[2]

The third item on the list of cons is probably advanced most often. Thus, some people who voted for #1 proclaimed that they "hate footnotes," probably on the theory that footnotes invariably require a downward glance. Not so — only when you need the numbers in order to pull out or pull up the authority.

The second con parallels the third, and so does the answer. Significant citational information need not be relegated to footnotes. Rather, the writer can — and usually should — provide the gist of the authority in the text. For instance: "The Michigan Trust Code provides . . ." or "But in 2009 the Sixth Circuit held . . ." or even "The leading case is *Harpo v. King Bee.*" Whatever the writer wishes to emphasize about the authority — or whatever the writer needs to introduce it or connect it analytically — can easily be put up front.

At any rate, if you're still not persuaded, at least read Garner's full argument on the subject.[3]

Let me now tell you the story behind my survey. In February [2010], I learned about a federal case in the Eastern District of Michigan called *Mosholder v Barnhardt*,[4] and more specifically about an opinion in that case denying the defendants' motion to dismiss or for summary judgment. All three examples marked #1 in the May column are from that opinion. And here's the stunner, from footnote 1 of the opinion:

> Defendant . . . followed what appears to be an Attorney General's office trend, citing every authority in a footnote. This practice is distracting to a reader and

---

[2]   *Id.*
[3]   *See, e.g., The Citational Footnote*, 7 Scribes J. Legal Writing 97 (1998–2000); *Clearing the Cobwebs from Judicial Opinions*, 38 Ct. Rev. 4 (Summer 2001), http://aja.ncsc.dni.us/courtrv/cr38-2/CR38-2Garner.pdf.
[4]   No. 09-CV-11829-DT (E.D. Mich. filed Feb. 12, 2010).

unacceptable to this judge. The Attorney General is notified that future filings in this judge's cases that confine case and statutory citations to footnotes will be stricken subject to refiling. Assistant Attorneys General Grill and Cabadas are directed to notify their supervisor(s) in writing of this point of procedure.[5]

Regardless of your vote or your opinion on footnoted citations, what do you think about an order like that? Page limits and type size and margins are one thing. They all go mainly to controlling length, although some court rules may bear on readability as well. But should individual judges be putting the brakes on a move to make legal papers more readable? Should they be stepping in on questions of formatting and style? Are they experts in these matters?

Now, the story has a mixed ending. The Office of the Attorney General has since reverted to putting citations in the text. Yet the case for footnoted citations is strong — as evidenced by a majority of readers who voted on side-by-side comparisons. They could see the improvement. That's the overriding message for writers who have a choice and who put a premium on clarity and readability.

[**Postscript.** Two points as this debate rages on. First, a reminder: any important "rhetorical" information — the court, date, case name — can be included in the text. Second, what about e-reading? Isn't it harder to scroll down for a citation than to glance down in print? Well, again, readers should have to glance down only in order to get the information needed to look up the citation. I suspect that just about everybody reads all the way through first and then returns to actually look up a handful of citations. People certainly don't stop and check each one as they read. So the question becomes whether the overall improvements in the text are

---

[5] Slip op. at 1.

offset by the need to scroll down for a selected number of citations.

No other professional writers continually interrupt their prose with full citations, often in strings. But change will be slow as long as judges resist it.]

The Best Test of a
New Lawyer's Writing

Let's say that your firm needs to hire a new lawyer. No small decision, and you don't want to go wrong, so you take the usual steps: sort applications, review transcripts, read writing samples, interview candidates, check references — and then pick someone from the short list. You might think that you have covered all the bases, but you would be wrong. You haven't done enough to assess the candidates' most important skill — their writing.

No one, I'm sure, will dispute that lawyers speak and write for a living. In a telling study by the American Bar Foundation, about 1,200 practicing lawyers were asked to rate lawyering skills from a list of 17 different skills. At the top of the list, in a class by themselves, were oral and written communication.[1] The American Bar Association has said the same thing, and in one report after another has encouraged, urged, pleaded with law schools to improve their legal-writing programs. One report, for instance, says, "Legal writing is at the heart of law practice, so it is especially vital that legal writing skills be developed and nurtured through carefully supervised instruction."[2]

To confirm how central writing is, look over the advertisements that appear in legal publications. In the latest issue of the *Michigan Lawyers Weekly* (as I prepare this 2010 [Plain Language] column), there are 18 ads under "Employment Available — Lawyer." As varied as the ads are, with

---

[1] Bryant G. Garth & Joanne Martin, *Law Schools and the Construction of Competence*, 43 J. Legal Educ. 469, 473, 477 (1993).

[2] Council of the Section of Legal Education and Admissions to the Bar, *Long-Range Planning for Legal Education in the United States* 29 (1987).

many seeking expertise in a specific practice area, 3 of them ask for a writing sample, and 6 others include statements like this:

- "Excellent written and oral communication skills are essential."
- "Desired: excellent writing ability."
- "Excellent writing and client skills are required."

When I did the identical experiment for the July 2001 column, those statements appeared in 10 of 26 ads. So nothing has changed. It's the same hiring pattern — the search for the same defining and distinguishing skill — week after week and year after year.

The Best Test: A Performance Test

What could be more obvious? To see what the candidates can do, have them do it. Once you get down to the short list of finalists, have each of them take a performance test — a writing exercise. The time and effort required of you and the candidates is piddling when compared with the investment that a decision to hire will entail. You can put the test together in a matter of hours, and then reuse it to your heart's content.

For the candidate, the performance test will take from two to six hours, depending on which test or tests you choose. At most, the candidate will have to spend a day at your office. If anyone seems to feel degraded or put upon by the test, that in itself might reveal something about the disposition of the person you would be working with.

Now, before turning to specifics, I want to explain that I'm talking mainly about testing a lawyer's ability to analyze and apply law in a clear and coherent way — to think straight on paper (or on a computer screen). At the same time, of course, you can assess the work in a general way for style and grammar. Is the writing tight, readable, and mostly error-free? You can decide how to weigh the different qualities and how much to forgive because of the time constraints. At any rate, you can bet on one thing: give a good performance test, and you will not hire a bad writer.

Here are the possibilities.

A Closed-World Performance Test

By "closed world," I mean that the writer does no research; you furnish the legal problem and the legal sources needed to address it.

A good example is the Multistate Performance Test, now administered in about 40 states. Candidates get a file — the factual background of a case, including relevant documents — and a library with the authorities they can use to analyze the legal issues. They have 90 minutes to write, for instance, a memorandum, a letter to the client, or a settlement proposal. You can allow more time if you want more polish.

Tests given in years past, along with the "point sheets," or answer guides, can be purchased quite reasonably from the National Conference of Bar Examiners. (Just go to the website.) Is it within bounds to use these ready-made tests for your own private performance test? Yes, it is, although the organization is obviously not trying to market its product that way.

As an alternative, you can easily create a closed-world test yourself.[3] You must have an office file that you can adapt. Put together a packet modeled on the Multistate Performance Test: an outline of facts, including the question you want answered and the instructions for what to write; perhaps a disputed document, a pleading, or excerpts from

---

[3]   See Ritchena Shepard, *Firm Exam Tests Writing Skills*, Nat'l L.J., Feb. 15, 1999, at A16 (noting that the Chicago firm of Connelly Sheehan Moran regards its test as the most important element of its hiring process).

depositions; the relevant statutes or rules; and not more than three or four cases. You could, as the multistate test sometimes does, include an irrelevant statute or case. Again, you have to assemble a packet just once. And presumably you have already done the analysis yourself, so you have a good idea of how the answer should go.

A Research-Added Performance Test

The only difference here is that you would not provide the selected library of legal authorities. You would provide only the file — whatever facts and documents you want the writer to use — and the writer would do the research, perhaps at your office (with access to electronic sources). I'd keep the research fairly basic. Adapt a file that you would give to a new lawyer — probably a one-issue state-law problem that does not involve more than one or two statutes and a few cases.

The research-added test should take about four hours, split into roughly three parts: researching, thinking and outlining, and writing. Or you could give it as an overnight take-home exercise if you wanted to put no premium on time.

A Test for Grammar and Style

You can find just such a test (complete with answers) in Volume 5 of *The Scribes Journal of Legal Writing*. The test, called "The Legal-Writing Skills Test," was devised by Bryan Garner. It has two parts: an editing section and an essay section. If you give one of the two performance tests described earlier, then skip the essays. The editing section has 35 items, most of them single sentences, that cover a range of skills: grammar and punctuation; correct usage (the difference between *affect* and *effect*, for example); converting the passive voice to the active voice; tightening wordy passages; and eliminating legalese. The editing test would add about 90 minutes.

In the end, you have to decide how important writing is in your practice, how confident you want to be about your decision, and what combination of tests to use.

Other Indicators of Writing Ability

There are traditional and obvious ways to gauge writing: look at what the candidates have already written or at the grades they earned in their required law-school writing classes. These credentials are worth considering, as long as you understand their not-so-obvious limitations.

A Writing Sample

A ten-page writing sample will probably involve a more complex analytical exercise than a performance exam does, so you can assess the writer's ability to handle a tougher intellectual challenge. Also, because the writer had the luxury of time, you won't wonder whether you should excuse deficiencies, and to what extent. The sample ought to be polished, and you can feel reasonably confident that it presents the writer at his or her best.

The trouble is, the sample may not be the writer's solitary best; it may be, at least to some extent, a collaborative effort. If it came from a legal-writing class, then it was probably critiqued (students would say "ripped") two or even three times — as a first draft, as a final draft, and possibly as a rewritten final draft. Moreover, it's not unheard of for students to ask a different writing professor to "look over" a writing sample before it departs into the real world. I've looked over my share in 30 years.

There's nothing wrong with any of this. Good writing instruction assumes good feedback, and the final product is still the writer's work, primarily. Just so you know.

A Published Article

Certainly, an article would be a plus. It tends to show intellectual ability, academic accomplishment, an interest in writing, advanced course work in writing, and the approval of other readers.

Again, though, you can't be sure how much editing the article needed or received from a scholarly-writing professor or from the journal's own editors. A portfolio item is not the same as a live performance.

One other suggestion: if the article inclines toward the plodding and overwrought style of most law journals, ask whether the writer can convert to the plain language that most readers strongly prefer in practice documents.[4] You might even pull a few pages from someone else's article and ask for a rewrite.

A Grade in a Law-School Writing Class

An A is good news and a C is bad news, but grades in between are harder to weigh unless you happen to know the program or the professor. Although a B+ looks good, maybe the professor gave no grade, or just a couple of grades, below a B. A C+ looks pretty bland, but maybe the candidate earned a better grade in a second required writing class. Then again, maybe the first professor was an experienced teacher and the second was not. There are many other variables. I would treat writing grades as one more indicator.

---

4   *See* Joseph Kimble, *Writing for Dollars, Writing to Please: The Case for Plain Language in Business, Government, and Law* 135–42, 151–54 (2012) (summarizing seven studies of legal readers).

Testing Yourself

Speaking of indicators, let me ask a few questions that I hope will not give you pause. But talented new lawyers do tell discouraging stories about the attitudes and practices of some supervisors.[5]

Do you resist, and maybe resent, the idea that lawyers ought to write in plain language? Do you regularly strain against the page limits that courts impose? Do you try to raise every issue imaginable, rather than settling for just your best ones? Do you wait a few pages before stating the issues and then state them superficially, rather than putting the deep issues up front?[6] Do you give a lengthy analysis of most cases, use lots of block quotations, and take few pains to make clear how each new case connects to the analysis and moves it forward?

Do your sentences average more than 20 words? Do you favor the passive voice and commonly turn verbs (like *consider*) into abstract nouns (*give consideration to*)? Do you end affidavits with "Further affiant sayeth naught"? Do you end contracts with "In witness whereof the parties hereto have affixed their signatures"? Are you fond of *prior to* and *in the event that* and *hereinafter*?

If you answered yes to any of these questions, you might look into a good book or seminar on legal writing — to help you judge writing smartly and mentor well.

---

[5] *See* Symposium, *The Politics of Legal Writing*, 7 Scribes J. Legal Writing 29 (1998–2000).

[6] *See* Bryan A. Garner, *Issue-Framing: The Upshot of It All*, Trial, Apr. 1997, at 74.

A Curious Criticism of Plain Language

Just when you thought you had answered every possible criticism of plain language, along comes one that you never could have imagined. The Fall 2015 issue of *Legal Communication & Rhetoric: JALWD* included an article called *Language Ideology and the Plain-Language Movement*, by Soha Turfler. The author, a lawyer who is now a doctoral student in Rhetoric and Writing, identifies what she describes as three "ideologies" from the movement and undertakes to "discuss how each ideology perpetuates discriminatory norms and practices."[1] Supposedly, advocates go wrong by promoting a prescriptive style, by trying to standardize language, and by thinking that plain language is morally superior to traditional legal style.

These three criticisms do not, however, hold up under any fair examination of what advocates actually say and do. I'll address each one after some initial comments.

Some Preliminary Points

Consider a few general observations about Turfler's article.

No Examples

The article does not contain a single example. It includes an appendix of assorted quotations — "considered [by the

---

[1] Soha Turfler, *Language Ideology and the Plain-Language Movement*, 12 Legal Communication & Rhetoric: JALWD 195, 198 (2015).

author] to be especially revealing"[2] — but not one example from the countless number that advocates have put forward for decades. Thus the article has an abstract, disembodied feel. Let's remember that the debate (legalese vs. plain language) is over differences like these:

Before:

One test that is helpful in determining whether or not a person was negligent is to ask and answer whether or not, if a person of ordinary prudence had been in the same situation and possessed of the same knowledge, he would have foreseen or anticipated that someone might have been injured by or as a result of his action or inaction. If such a result from certain conduct would be foreseeable by a person of ordinary prudence with like knowledge and in like situation, and if the conduct reasonably could be avoidable, then not to avoid it would be negligence.

After:

To decide whether the defendant was negligent, there is a test you can use. Consider how a reasonably careful person would have acted in the same situation. To find the defendant negligent, you would have to answer "yes" to the following two questions:

(1) Would a reasonably careful person have realized in advance that someone might be injured by the defendant's conduct?

(2) Could a reasonably careful person have avoided behaving as the defendant did?

If your answer to both of these questions is "yes," then the defendant was negligent. You can use the same test in deciding whether the plaintiff was negligent.

---

[2] *Id.* at 200.

Before:

When two or more statements are made in the alternative and one of them if made independently would be sufficient, the pleading is not made insufficient by the insufficiency of one or more of the alternative statements.

After:

If a party makes alternative statements, the pleading is sufficient if any one of them is sufficient.

No Mention of the Evidence

The article ignores the evidence that plain language works. The author cites my book *Writing for Dollars, Writing to Please* many times, but she never mentions the 50 case studies summarized in Part Five. They involved many different kinds of documents and settings. As those studies demonstrate, readers strongly prefer plain language to legalese and officialese, understand it better and faster, are more likely to read it in the first place, and are more likely to comply with it. Without countering that empirical evidence, the author baldly asserts: "Plain style is . . . no[t] more consistently effective . . . than other styles."[3] Yes, it is.

A Narrow Definition

The author circumscribes plain language in describing it: "such features as active voice, short sentences, and familiar words";[4] "[avoiding] specific language features — such as obscure Latin terms or long, periodic sentences";[5] "[f]or example, one common prescription is to use familiar or to avoid obsolete words."[6] Even as she acknowledges that "advocates

---

[3]   *Id.* at 198.
[4]   *Id.* at 196.
[5]   *Id.* at 201.
[6]   *Id.* at 203.

. . . often rely on various lists of rules and preferences,"[7] she tends to reduce plain language to simple words and short, active sentences. It's much more than that, as she must know.

I listed more than 40 guidelines in *Writing for Dollars, Writing to Please* (pp. 5–10). They span everything from design, organization, sentences, and words to general principles like testing consumer documents on typical readers. And I prefaced the list with a qualification: "Of course, bare guidelines are not enough: they need to be explained and illustrated, and applied with an eye for possible exceptions and occasional tensions between them." In short, the guidelines are flexible and varied. The author loses sight of all that in suggesting that advocates are bent on "a singular style as the standard for all written discourse."[8]

Almost No Useful Advice

Throughout her article, Turfler plumbs sociolinguistic theory and its jargon: *the methodology of linguistic differentiation, communicative action, macrosocial constraints, iconicity, recursiveness, erasure, heterogeneity, linguistic revalorization.* Now, plain-language advocates have always welcomed insights from linguistic and cognitive disciplines. We're eager to learn, of course. But after studiously reading this exploration, I'm not sure what to *do* with it.

The author encourages everyone "to examine the three ideologies discussed below and to consider how to improve legal discourse."[9] Toward the end, she says that advocates could "focus their efforts on revising the ways that . . . legal discourse is structured, and find means to reject unfair and discriminatory hierarchies in which certain ways of using language are more valued than others."[10] It would be helpful to know how she would improve legal discourse. What

---

[7] *Id.*
[8] *Id.* at 197.
[9] *Id.* at 198.
[10] *Id.* at 215.

(more) can be done to make it fair to lawyers, clients, judges, and other people who have to deal with legal documents?

But no one should think that all styles are equally good, clear, effective, and (yes) valued by readers generally. Just about everyone who has ever taught or given advice about legal writing believes otherwise, and the evidence supports them in counseling against legalese.

Various Inaccuracies

The article includes some misstatements, overstatements, and murky connections that create a false impression about plain-language work and advocates. Three bulleted examples follow.

- [T]he Plain Language movement associates specific language features — such as obscure Latin terms or long periodic sentences — with legalese and then uses these associations to make social evaluations about the group that uses such features. . . . Traditional legal writers are characterized as "wordy, stuffy, artificial, and often ungrammatical" individuals . . . .[11]

Notice how the internal quotation (from Bryan Garner) ends before the word *individuals*, which the author added. Garner was not criticizing lawyers as individuals, as people. Nor was he making a "social evaluation" about lawyers or the legal profession. He was criticizing their tendencies as legal writers — that is, the way they perform one aspect of their job. If studies show that doctors tend to interrupt patients or not listen carefully, are the researchers making "social evaluations" or moral judgments about doctors? Or are they trying to solve a problem? And by the way, how can individuals be "ungrammatical"? It's about the writing, not the person.

---

[11] *Id.* at 201.

- [A]dvocates often distinguish plain style by its reli-
ance on active voice; yet these same advocates recognize that they sometimes use passive constructions,
nevertheless explaining that passive voice is used only
when necessary and appropriate. On the other hand,
passive voice is considered overused, unnecessary, and
inappropriate when used in legalese. In this way, the
Plain Language movement can legitimatize the use
of certain stylistic features in its own styles and dis-
courses, while stigmatizing legalese when it relies on
the very same features.[12]

Did you follow the logic of that? Nobody considers the
passive unnecessary or inappropriate *when* used in legalese.
Rather, its overuse may be symptomatic *of* legalese — one
possible symptom among many others. The style doesn't
characterize the features; the features characterize the style.
You might as well accuse advocates of saying that *pursuant
to* and *further affiant sayeth naught* are quite appropriate
when used in a plain style. The author needs to explain why
a guideline like "prefer the active voice" — together with a
list of exceptions or good uses of the passive — is somehow
bad advice. The same goes for all the other plain-language
guidelines.

- [T]he concept of audience often offers little help in defining "familiar" words when it comes to legal texts.
But the Plain Language movement mostly erases this
heterogeneity, relying instead on homogenous con-
cepts to define its features.[13]

Usually, the same plain language works for most people.
For most readers (if not all), isn't *I have received* more
likely to be easily understood than *the undersigned hereby
acknowledges receipt of*? Any guideline has to be stated more
or less generally. Yet even then, one of the most important

---

[12] *Id.* at 202.
[13] *Id.* at 204.

guidelines is to test consumer documents with a small group of typical users whenever possible.[14] We want to know whether they indeed understand the words in the document.

To support her point about "erasure" of "heterogeneity," the author cites an article recommending a seventh-grade reading level for texts. But surely she knows that readability formulas are controversial and that most advocates either don't recommend them at all or recommend them only as one way of assessing clarity (or, more accurately, lack of clarity).

I could continue in this vein, but let's turn to the three language myths and the related ideologies that plain language supposedly perpetuates.

The Myth of Decay and the Problems with Prescription

What are plain-language advocates guilty of, according to Turfler? Believing that the language is in a state of deterioration. Trying to purify or control language use. Offering an incontestable cure. Not recognizing that language changes and that lawyers have over time molded the law into a discourse called legalese. Being an elite group with a moral duty to pronounce on language behavior. Being a prescriptive movement.[15]

A state of decay and deterioration? No, we believe that most legal writing has been pretty awful for centuries, and scholars agree.[16]

Trying to purify and control language use? No, trying to improve it, for the sake of readers. The author uses the lan-

---

[14] *Federal Plain Language Guidelines* 100–12 (2011), http://www.plainlanguage .gov/howto/guidelines/FederalPLGuidelines/FederalPLGuidelines.pdf.

[15] Turfler, 12 JALWD at 205–08.

[16] *See, e.g.*, David Mellinkoff, *The Language of the Law* 24 (1963) (concluding, from an exhaustive historical study, that legal language has a strong tendency to be "wordy, unclear, pompous, and dull").

guage of authoritarianism to discredit a reform movement. Inevitably, some of our guidelines sound like dictates — "omit unnecessary words" — but they are in the nature of advice, suggestions, recommendations.

As for not recognizing that language changes, we are not so benighted. In fact, *Garner's Modern English Usage* (4th ed. 2016) includes a "language-change index" that tries to measure, in five stages, the changing usage of different words and phrases. The author cites no advocate — not one — who holds the view that language is fixed.

Not recognizing that the law has been molded into a discourse called legalese? Indeed it has, and that's the trouble. We acknowledge that the law, like any other profession, has certain terms of art, although (in my view, at least) they are more rare and more replaceable than lawyers like to think.[17] Beyond that, the author needs to provide some examples of how this highly developed discourse serves both the public and the profession. Try to find readers and commentators who approve of the state of legal writing and drafting. For every one she finds, I'll give you many more who castigate it, including judges and lawyers themselves.[18]

Finally, the charge of prescriptivism. The author sprinkles her criticism with vocabulary like this: "notions of legitimacy or correctness," "imposition of a singular style," "claim the right to control the communicative practices of an entire community," "a select few self-appointed authorities."[19]

The readers of *JALWD* are mainly legal-writing teachers. Has any one of you ever put a passage on the board or screen, asked your students to rewrite it, settled on a different

---

[17] *See* this book at 17–19; *see also* Kimble, *Writing for Dollars, Writing to Please: The Case for Plain Language in Business, Government, and Law* 35–37 (2012) (discussing why plain language is not subverted by the need to use technical terms).

[18] *See, e.g.*, Bryan A. Garner, *Learning to Loathe Legalese*, Mich. B.J., Nov. 2006, at 52; Garner, *Judges on Effective Writing: The Importance of Plain Language*, Mich. B.J., Feb. 2005, at 44.

[19] Turfler, 12 JALWD at 205, 206, 207, 208.

version, and asked, "Which is better, clearer, more effective, more persuasive?" Has any one of you ever offered what you regarded as a model, an exemplar, of a certain piece of writing? I wouldn't call that being rigid, elitist, prescriptive, controlling. I'd call it teaching your students how to better communicate with their readers.

The Myth of Homogeneity and the Problems with Standardization

Before I get to the next volleys, an observation: in this section of her article, the author (again) does not cite one plain-language advocate who makes the kinds of assertions that she accuses advocates of making. Not one, in 20 footnotes.

So what are these next accusations? Advocates believe in "standard-language ideology"; "seek[] to erase linguistic variety by establishing norms and standards in which some usages are accepted as legitimate and others are stigmatized"; and assert that "anyone who uses language improperly should be excluded or corrected."[20]

Exactly the opposite is true. The central goal of the plain-language movement is to include, not exclude. It seeks to make legal and official writing clear and accessible to the greatest possible number of intended readers. Anyone who reads the literature, follows the discussion groups, and attends the conferences knows about the concern that advocates have to reach low-literacy and other readers with various challenges. The Plain Language Commission, for example, recently published the second edition of a free book called *Communicating with Older People*.[21] As just one more example, a plenary speaker at the 2015 conference

---

[20]   *Id.* at 208.
[21]   Sara Carr, *Communicating with Older People: Writing in Plain English* (2d ed. 2016), www.clearest.co.uk/books.

of the Plain Language Association International gave a talk called "e-Accessibility: Leaving No One Behind Online," about designing websites for people with disabilities. He approached the podium wearing goggles that dimmed vision, and passed the goggles around so that people could see for themselves. If you think that plain language is exclusionary, look through the program for that conference.[22]

What's more, as already noted, a basic tenet of plain language is that mass documents, public documents, should be tested with typical readers to make sure that they will be intelligible and useful to the intended audience.[23] And we try to keep abreast of research to determine whether the guidelines (not rules; not fixed, immutable norms) are supported by evidence.[24]

It rings hollow, then, to say that "the [plain-language] ideology encourages a view of 'language as a relatively fixed, invariant and unchanging entity.'"[25] And it borders on offensiveness to suggest that advocates wish to "force[] nonconforming individuals into either identity-stripping assimilation . . . or further marginalization."[26] Likewise to say that "the Plain Language movement comes dangerously close to promoting a system which favors, legitimatizes, and promotes individuals from privileged groups and which disfavors, stigmatizes, and marginalizes others."[27] The author

---

[22] http://Plain2015.ie/wp-content/uploads/2015/10/PLAIN2015 _Programme_ Final.pdf.

[23] *See, e.g.*, International Plain Language Federation, *What Is Plain Language?*, http://plainlanguagenetwork.org/plain-language/what-is-plain-language ("A communication is in plain language if the language, structure, and design are so clear that the intended audience can easily find what they need, understand what they find, and use that information.").

[24] *See* Karen A. Schriver, *Developing Plain-Language Guidelines Internationally*, YouTube (June 24, 2015), https://www.youtube.com/watch? v=10B1bYIu5us.

[25] Turfler, 12 JALWD at 209 (citation omitted).

[26] *Id*. at 210.

[27] *Id*. at 211.

mistakes the tone and purpose and actual effect of plain language. I've yet to hear about any group that feels stigmatized by best efforts at clarity, and the author cites no examples or evidence. It's all theory, and elusive at that.

This paragraph is typical:

> Plain language, of course, relies on the rules of Standard American English. Thus, the imposition of plain-language standards will not increase access to justice for groups already marginalized by this dialect. This is true regardless of whether plain style actually has the potential to make the law more understandable to individuals who lack legal training. Nonstandard-language speakers may not have access to the resources that would allow them to understand these standard texts, no matter how plainly they are written.[28]

Well, yes, most plain-language documents in the United States are in standard English. Where else would you start? But many are in Spanish. Many are in other languages to meet the needs of those speakers. (For example, information about voting in Los Angeles County is available in ten different languages.[29]) Around the world, advocates are working to meet the language needs of audiences in their countries.[30] And despite all that, we're criticized for marginalizing those we don't manage to reach?

It is legal style that marginalizes people, even those who are proficient in standard English. It is legal style that "prescribes" old models from one generation to the next. It is legal style that has been standardized — in an archaic, dense,

---

[28] *Id.* at 210.
[29] *See* Los Angeles County Registrar-Recorder/County Clerk, *Voter Bill of Rights*, https://lavote.net/documents/materials_voter_bill_of_rights.pdf.
[30] *See, e.g., Plain Language Around the World*, Plain Language Association International, http://plainlanguagenetwork.org/plain-language/plain-language-around-the-world (listing organizations and resources in many different countries and languages).

verbose language that most people simply cannot understand.

The Myth of Superiority and the Problems of Morality

From an article in the journal *Clarity* reviewing several
ways to define plain language, the author pulls a paragraph
suggesting that the need for honesty should be incorporated into the standards (guidelines) set for plain-language
practitioners and documents.[31] Why? Because a lie can be
expressed in plain language.

But an honesty component does not appear in any of the
definitions or guidelines discussed at length in the *Clarity*
article. It has never played a significant part in the modern
push for plain language. Maybe it should, but it hasn't. The
author is treating a possibility as if it were a pillar.

Next accusation:

> [L]egalese is often portrayed as morally deficient
> puffery designed to manipulate and deceive, or as the
> intentional obfuscation of language for the purposes
> of maintaining current the hierarchy wherein lawyers
> possess unchallenged authority over legal discourse.[32]

As an example of someone who has so "portrayed" legal
language, the author cites me, or rather my book *Writing
for Dollars, Writing to Please*, adding in a parenthetical that
I was "reviewing [the] argument that lawyers have a 'vested
interest in obscurity.'"[33] But wait — I was addressing a hy-
pothetical defense of legalese that some lawyers *might* make,
not portraying legalese as "morally deficient." I was not describing legalese but criticizing those who would defend it
out of naked self-interest.

---

[31] Turfler, 12 JALWD at 212.

[32] *Id.*

[33] *Id.* n.96.

I went on to say that "I think very few [lawyers], when pressed, would argue for deliberate obscurity. There's no vast conspiracy to perpetuate legalese."[34] So, far from portraying legalese as an exercise in "the intentional obfuscation of language," I said just the opposite: "[Legalese] keeps its hold on many lawyers, sadly, for the reasons discussed in the previous section (inertia, habit, overreliance on old models, a misunderstanding of plain language, lack of training and self-awareness, and the specter of too little time)."[35] None of these has to do with intentional obfuscation.

Next, the author says that the plain-language movement's "moral concerns about language use are not new."[36] She then quotes two sociolinguists for the proposition that "language guardians often portray certain styles and usages as signs of 'stupidity, ignorance, perversity, moral degeneracy, etc.'"[37] Thus is the charge of "moral concerns" — which is tenuous to begin with — equated with labeling some writers as "stupid" and "ignorant." Once again, the author does not cite an advocate who uses terms or a tone like that. And if we have suggested that clinging to legalese is perverse, it's not in any sense of being dishonest or immoral, but of being stubborn or closed-minded.

Then the author refers to "the fuzzy distinctions between legalese and plain style."[38] She ignores an extensive body of literature — several decades' worth — that identifies the characteristics of legalese, provides guidelines for plain style, and illustrates the difference.[39]

And so on, and so on:

---

[34] Kimble, *Writing for Dollars, Writing to Please* at 28.
[35] *Id.* at 28–29.
[36] Turfler, 12 JALWD at 212.
[37] *Id.*
[38] *Id.* at 213.
[39] *See, e.g.,* this book at 35–126.

- [T]hese complaints and concerns are an assessment of the relative moral merit or truthfulness of the users of these various styles.[40]

We're going in circles. As pointed out earlier, the concern is with the quality and effectiveness of the writing, not the character of the person. Someone who wastes a reader's time may be thoughtless or unproficient or overtaxed, but he or she is not immoral, not a bad person.

- [T]he belief that legal discourse is in need of correction may be a belief that the legal profession and laws are in need of moral realignment, or at least superficial revision.[41]

These are two very different things: substantive change and stylistic revision. The author knows which one advocates are focused on.

- By diverting attention towards stylistic revision, the Plain Language movement arguably inhibits substantive reforms that could actually address [the moral and social failings of our legal system].[42]

Do we, then, just forget about the enormous inefficiencies of poor communication in the legal profession? Forget about whether people can understand all the information, important to their lives, that comes from business and government as well? Shrug off the huge waste of time and money, the confusion and ill-will and distrust, the recurring cry for clarity in public discourse? The author's argument, it seems, is that we have more important things to attend to.

You readers can judge for yourselves whether clear, plain writing is worth the candle. I'll leave it at that.

---

[40] Turfler, 12 JALWD at 213.

[41] *Id.*

[42] *Id.* at 214.

PART THREE

Interviews and Remarks

Interview in *Bimonthly Review of Law Books*

This interview appeared in the July–August 2006 issue. (The Bimonthly Review of Law Books *is no longer published.) The interview was prompted by my (then) new book* Lifting the Fog of Legalese: Essays on Plain Language. *The interviewer was Michael Rustad, the coeditor.*

MR: Your law school is named after Justice Thomas M. Cooley, former Michigan Supreme Court Justice and a treatise writer in the grand style.

JK: I'm not a Cooley scholar, but I have browsed through a couple of his books. I wouldn't say that he had a crisp or conversational style. As you suggest, his style — consistent with the style of his day — was more elevated than you might see in the best contemporary writers. A simple example: "A law is sometimes said to be unconstitutional, by which is meant that it is opposed to the principles or rules of the constitution of the state." I might write: "A law is sometimes said to be unconstitutional — meaning that it violates the principles or rules of the state constitution." And his sentences tended to be longer, on average, and more winding than I would write. But on the whole, Cooley's writing was clear and free from unnecessary jargon. And I'm pleased to note that he regularly started sentences with *And*, *But*, and *So*.

MR: What do you see as the principal writing problems of entering law students? What steps can entering law students take to avoid overblown legalese?

JK: I'm sure that the problems are pretty much the same as
      they have always been. Back in 1939, in an article called
      English as She Is Wrote, William Prosser lamented that
      "very, very many" of his students were "hopelessly,
      deplorably unskilled and inept in the use of words to
      say what they mean or, indeed, to say anything at all."
      (Later, after changing schools, he said the situation at
      his new school was not quite as bad.) Now, what are
      the principal problems? Writing coherently so that the
      ideas connect. That might be the big one. Too often, I
      can't follow the line of thought. Then writing clearly
      and simply, so I can easily understand the particular
      point. Then getting the mechanics right. It's not one
      problem, really. Students who are deficient in some
      aspect are usually deficient in others. The underlying
      cause, I think, is that many students have not read
      enough, written enough, or been critiqued enough.
      They have not made a habit of attending to words.

      Of course, you hear the same complaint in other fields.
      But law students are entering a verbal profession —
      lawyers are professional writers — so we can't just
      throw up our hands and blame the high schools and
      colleges. Law schools have to provide rigorous writing
      programs so that their students get better. And, in-
      deed, most schools have strengthened their programs
      in the last 10 to 15 years. The trends are in the right
      direction.

MR: What steps can entering law students take to avoid
      overblown legalese?

JK: First, inoculate yourself. Realize that the opinions
      you read every day are probably not models of good
      writing. Don't try to imitate their style. Second, listen
      to your writing professors. Most of them are commit-
      ted to purging legalese. Third, read Richard Wydick's
      Plain English for Lawyers or Bryan Garner's *Legal*

Writing in Plain English. Fourth, get over the idea that jargon and highfalutin language are signs of a great mind. Strive for simplicity — without oversimplifying. Finally, realize that writing well is a lifelong job that requires constant attention and practice.

MR: If you were appointed to teach at a school for new judges, what would you tell newly appointed jurists about writing better judicial opinions?

JK: There's an essay in my book called *The Straight Skinny on Better Judicial Opinions*. I actually tested an opinion. I gave readers an O and a Y version. O was the original and Y was the revised version, although I didn't tell readers that. The result: 39% of readers preferred the original, and 61% preferred the revised version, which followed plain-language principles. I also asked readers why they preferred O or Y. For readers who chose Y, the top reason was that it left out a lot of unnecessary detail. And the next reason was that it had a summary at the beginning. In the essay, I examine the differences between the two versions and even edit the original.

Incidentally, in another essay, called *First Things First: The Lost Art of Summarizing*, I discuss the importance of summaries and what makes for an effective one. I took a random volume of the *Michigan Reports*, read every opinion, and concluded that only 9 of the 27 in that volume used an effective summary at the beginning. The essay includes a bunch of examples.

MR: Why do you single out the SEC in your open letter in your book?

JK: At the time, the SEC was considering a rule to require plain English in certain parts of prospectuses. Of course, the SEC was hearing all the usual false criticisms of plain language — that it's not precise, that it doesn't allow for technical terms, that it's too subjective to enforce, and so on. So I published an open letter in the *Michigan Bar Journal* supporting the rule.

MR: What are your recommendations for the five or six best books on legal writing?

JK: Well, I've already mentioned the books by Wydick and Garner. Certainly, you can't go wrong with any of Garner's books. But in a way, I hate to mention some books because I'll leave out other good ones. My book includes an Appendix 2, called "A Plain-Language Bookshelf," in which I list 4 indispensable guides to usage and style, more than 25 good books on plain writing, and 2 valuable journals (*Clarity* and *The Scribes Journal of Legal Writing*).

MR: How does your new book compare with Bryan Garner's book on writing a persuasive brief?

JK: *The Winning Brief* is superb, and not many books compare with it. Mine is more eclectic; it's a collection of essays. I include empirical evidence about plain language from the testing I've done. I address (and I hope explode) the terrible, stubborn myths about plain language, as well as the excuses for traditional style. I use some high-profile examples — the orders in the Clinton impeachment trial and part of the USA Patriot Act — to illustrate the bad and the good. And I try to provide some inspiration and some writing advice along the way.

MR: Why do judges have so many problems with jury instructions, given that model jury instructions are so readily available? What are some of the pitfalls you've seen in model instructions, based on your own experience as a consultant in Michigan?

JK: The word *model* doesn't necessarily mean "good." We have standard, or pattern, instructions in most jurisdictions, but many of them are appalling. We might as well be speaking to jurors in Greek. And people's lives may literally depend on instructions. What an indictment — that when we have to communicate with the public, we so often make a hash of it.

Why? Again, I address some of the reasons in the essay *How to Mangle Court Rules and Jury Instructions*. For instance, we don't treat accuracy and clarity as equally important. (I'm convinced from experience that striving for clarity also improves accuracy.) Too often, we slavishly follow the exact language of statutes and opinions. We don't let a writing expert prepare the first draft. We have traditionally neglected legal drafting in law school. There are lots of reasons. But the winds of change are blowing. You may have heard about California's huge project to rewrite all its civil and criminal instructions in plain English. Some other states have done or are doing the same.

As for the pitfalls, you can guess my answer: the instructions are not written in plain language. I don't just mean that they use long, involved sentences and unfamiliar words. I mean that they violate dozens of guidelines for writing clearly. Besides that, they ignore some other principles that would improve instructions in particular — principles that usually don't apply to other forms of drafting. For instance, use questions, use controlled repetition, state things in alternative ways.

MR: You single out the Patriot Act as an example of poor drafting. What drafting problems did you see with the Act?

JK: I list 12 kinds of small-scale deficiencies, without even getting into format, organization, sentence structure, and the like. An aversion to pronouns. An aversion to possessives. Ten others. I try to identify some of the persistent, inexcusable failings that pervade not just drafting but all legal writing. Good stylists or editors would fix these things almost routinely. And the great irony is that most lawyers consider themselves rather good writers; it's everybody else's writing that needs work.

MR: I was wondering whether you have any theories about why bad writing continues to thrive. I have recently reviewed a large number of arbitration agreements intended for nursing homes. Few of these agreements make any attempt to explain arbitration or its proce-dures. Do you have any explanation why so many top corporate attorneys are so determined to avoid writing in a clear, concise, or specific way? My private theory is that the fog of legalese deliberately keeps consumers in the dark. Do you have an opinion on the cause of unclear writing in so many consumer contracts?

JK: I don't think it's a conspiracy. I think there are various reasons: the overwhelming influence of poor models, not enough good training at all stages of schooling, a tendency (especially among law students) to overrate oral skills and underrate written skills, false notions of prestige, a general lack of self-awareness, and simple inertia — to name some of the more obvious ones. If you want to boil it down, lack of will and lack of skill.

MR: Tell our readers a little about your experience editing *The Scribes Journal of Legal Writing.*

JK: I'd like to write an article about that — an editor's pleasure and pain. I'm the editor in chief among four veterans. [Since 2012, I've been senior editor; the cur-rent editor in chief is Mark Cooney.] I think many legal writers are not used to having their work marked up by seasoned editors. Once in a great while, an author becomes angry. Sometimes authors resist what seem to be obvious improvements. Then you have the author who doesn't want to use dashes or hyphenate phrasal (compound) adjectives or use contractions. But there are ways of handling the process and working out the differences. Most of our authors are very grateful — and say so.

MR: If legal writing is so critical to the law-school mission, why has legal writing been so marginalized in the curriculum?

JK: I'm afraid it comes down to money. Any of the skills courses — legal writing, trial practice, a clinic — require more resources than the doctrinal courses.

MR: What steps has WMU–Cooley taken to help students develop plain-writing skills?

JK: Some of the ways: (1) Cooley was the first law school to put its writing teachers on tenure track and keep them there, so our students are generally taught by veteran profs. (2) As part of the hiring process, we ask candidates to write comments on a student paper. A performance test, if you will. The results are revealing. (3) We teach the first writing course in the second term, not the first term. That's rather heretical, but I think students are so overwhelmed by the new subject matter that skills are harder to teach at the very beginning. And there's the matter of time: students grumble about how much time the writing courses take. I ask them to imagine how they would have managed in the first term. (4) We teach two other required courses, including one in the last year, trying to bridge between the earlier courses and entry into practice. The lessons from the first year are, sadly, too soon forgotten. (5) We require legal drafting (contracts, statutes, etc.) as part of our program. The legalese is thickest in legal drafting — more than in the other forms of legal writing (briefs, memos) — so we can attack it at its worst. (6) Above all, our Research and Writing Department is strongly committed to teaching clarity and simplicity. We make no bones about it.

MR: What is your primary audience for *Lifting the Fog of Legalese?*

JK: Lawyers and law students. But I think that any government or business writer could also benefit from it.

MR: How can practicing attorneys benefit from your book?

JK: For those who doubt the value of plain language, I
hope to open their eyes and move them off dead center.
For those who want to improve their writing, I hope
they will find some useful advice and examples. I even
hope that the essays are enjoyable to read — and, as I
said, provide a little inspiration.

Interview in *Issues in Writing*

This interview appeared in Volume 15, Spring–Summer 2005. The interviewers were the editors, Mary Bowman, Dan Dieterich, Wade Mahon, and Sarah Pogell of the University of Wisconsin–Stevens Point.

Eds: How did you first get interested in plain language for lawyers?

JK: It was more or less by accident. It didn't hit me when I was in law school that something was terribly wrong with all these opinions that I was reading — the steady diet of legal writing that law students are fed every day. It hit me when I was at one of my early jobs in the '70s. I was on the staff of the Michigan Supreme Court, and I was assigned to write rules of procedure for the Michigan courts. I thought to myself, "I don't have a clue." I mean, I'd barely had a writing course in law school. We wrote one brief supervised by third-year students, and we got a little introduction to the library. That was the extent of our training in legal writing.

And so when I was assigned to write court rules for the Michigan Supreme Court, I went down to the library. There was one book on legal drafting. I got that book — *The Fundamentals of Legal Drafting*, by Reed Dickerson — and started thumbing through it. I came across a section that said on one side of the page, "Don't say this" and on the other side of the page, "Instead consider," or something like that. That sort of turned on the light. I thought, "Man, there *is* a lot of inflated stuff in legal writing." And from there my interest has grown.

As an English major in college, I always had an interest in writing and language. If it didn't strike somebody like me in law school, imagine how unlikely it would be to strike most law students from a different background.

Eds: What is your view of the status of the plain-language movement? Are people in other countries more or less interested in it than we in the U.S. are?

JK: I think that of all the countries, Australia may be out front on this. It has been for the last 10 or 15 years. Why? Just because they had some active people who were in a position to do something, to work with some of the bigger law firms in Australia, work on some of the government projects, and so on, and it just seemed to take off in Australia in a way that it hasn't in some other countries.[1]

But it's hard for me to say where we're at in the U.S. For one reason, you know, I'm in an academic environment. I was in practice for a while, but I don't see as many briefs or other kinds of legal documents as I used to, so it's a little hard for me to judge. Besides that, I move in plain-language circles and attend plain-language conferences and writing conferences, so I suppose that that probably colors my view a little bit. But I like to think that there's increased awareness of plain language among lawyers. I have to think that; otherwise, my professional life has been for naught. I've been beating my brains out for 20 years. If it hasn't done any good, that would be a little discouraging.

---

[1] For an updated and expanded perspective on historical developments in plain language worldwide, see Part Four of Joseph Kimble, *Writing for Dollars, Writing to Please: The Case for Plain Language in Business, Government, and Law* (2012).

I think there has been a slow, incremental, cumulative effect from the initiatives that have come and gone over the last 10 or 15 years. President Clinton issued a plain-language memorandum, and Al Gore was involved in the reinventing-government project. Many of the federal workers who were involved in that are still active in the federal government. So you had the Clinton–Gore initiative. The Securities and Exchange Commission is still supporting plain language too. And we have a new Center for Plain Language in Washington, D.C. I was one of the founding directors of that, but some of the other directors are persons who were involved in the Clinton–Gore effort. We have a nice website, www.plainlanguage.gov, a good resource for people who are interested in the subject.

There's an international community working on plain language. The Plain Language Association International has a conference every other year. In fact, we just had the fifth one in Washington, D.C. They've got a great website, www.plainlanguagenetwork.org. I'm involved in Clarity, which is an international association started by lawyers. We have about a thousand members worldwide and a country representative, an agent so to speak, in more than 25 countries. We also publish *The Clarity Journal* twice a year. Back issues are available on our website, www .clarity-international.net.

Finally, there's the Scribes organization, which publishes *The Scribes Journal of Legal Writing*, and that journal has a pretty strong plain-language slant or viewpoint. So there are a lot of groups and publications, and a lot of persons who are interested in it.

The question is, "Has it made a dent in the mountain of legalese?" I just don't have a good feel for that. I'm hopeful because in the last 10 or 15 years, most law schools have tried to improve their legal-writing programs. When I was in law school, there wasn't a required legal-writing course. Now most law schools devote at least a couple of courses to it, and some devote even more. Most are taught by full-time professors rather than adjuncts. And so I'm hopeful that more and more young lawyers are exposed to plain language and the principles of clear writing in law school. That will have an effect as time goes on.

I'm sure, though, that most legal papers are still too long and too dense. We are fighting 400 years of tradition when it comes to poor legal writing. So that's kind of an "I'm not certain, but I'm hopeful" answer.

Eds: What do you see your role in the plain-language movement to be?

JK: Besides teaching my students, I've gravitated to trying to deal with two or three aspects of this. I've tried to address the myths about plain language in my writing because these are the "Yeah, but . . ." arguments that I got originally from my students and that I still get from other lawyers. "Well, yeah, plain language is all well and good, but what about this or that?"

If I were to list some of these myths briefly, one would be that plain language is really a matter of baby talk or dumbing down the language. Two, plain language is just about simple words and short sentences. Three, plain language is not precise, and legal writing has to be very precise. Of course, I turn that argument around. I say that plain language is more precise than traditional legal style because it lays bare all the uncertainties and inconsistencies and ambiguities that traditional legal style, with all its excesses, tends to hide. So I say that plain language is more precise than traditional legal style. Of course we can write precisely and clearly — a lot better than we lawyers have traditionally tended to do.

What are some other myths about plain language? What about technical terms? Don't lawyers have to use technical terms? Well, yes, lawyers have to use technical terms, but 98% of the words in legal documents are not technical; 1 or 2% of the words are. We've actually tested some legal documents, and we find that in a standard contract, 1 to 3% of the words are what you might call technical terms, but the rest could be written in plain language.

So that's first: I've tried to deal with some of these myths about what it means to write in plain language. I've also tried to respond to the question, "How do I know that this is acceptable?" or (mostly from my students) "How do I know that this is acceptable out in the real world?" I started testing legal documents on readers. I've done this three or four times now. I've been involved in several rounds of testing, and I've found out that lawyers and judges prefer to read a clear, plain document rather than a document that's written in traditional style. And the evidence on this is very strong.

Well, okay, so everybody wants the other person's prose to be plain, right? But then, of course, when lawyers sit down to write their own legal papers, they forget that. They forget the golden rule: "Write for your reader. Write how you want your reader to write for you." It's a huge disconnect. Anyway, I've tried to help develop the empirical evidence that even legal readers, let alone your average members of the public, prefer to read plain language.

The other area I've concentrated on is trying to collect empirical data on the benefits of plain language. These are some really staggering numbers. Some studies out there have tested the value of plain language and tried to estimate the cost savings from using it in

government and business documents. In "Writing for
Dollars, Writing to Please,"[2] published in *The Scribes
Journal of Legal Writing*, I collected 20 or so studies of
this kind. To take an example, the Veterans Adminis-
tration revised a letter that it sends out to veterans and
then had the telephone operators at one of its regional
offices keep track of the number of phone calls they
got about that letter in one year. Before the letter was
revised, they were getting about 1,200 calls a year. After the letter was revised, they were getting 200 calls
a year. Imagine! This is just one letter tested in one
regional office of one government agency. Multiply
that by all the letters, forms, fliers, notices, and pieces
of information that every division and department of
every government agency sends out to the public all
the time. It's incredible.

I think that poor communication is the great hidden
cost — the great hidden waste in business and government. And so that's the other area I try to concentrate
on. I try to collect the work that's been done on this by
other people.

That's been my role: exposing the myths, doing some
testing to show that readers prefer plain language, and
trying to collect some of the empirical evidence about
the value of plain language versus legalese and officialese. Of course, I've also tried to write a little bit about
the how-tos of plain language.

Eds: Why are lawyers unclear in their writing?

JK: Some people think that this is a conspiracy among
     lawyers — that lawyers do this deliberately to mys-
     tify the public and somehow make people dependent
     on lawyers. I really don't think it is any sort of con-
     scious conspiracy. I think it's a combination of things.

---

2   Now incorporated into Part Five of the book, which summarizes 50 studies
     on the extraordinary benefits of plain language.

Basically, it comes down to a lack of will and lack of skill.

I played a lot of golf when I was growing up. I would stand out there on the practice tee and the pro would wander by (I was good friends with the pro), and I would say to him, "I just can't seem to draw the ball! Why can't I hit it with a little draw on it?" He would say, "Lack of skill." And that's it: lack of will and lack of skill.

Now, to be a little more specific: besides inertia, you have things like poor training, overreliance on poor models and forms, and bad habits. I mean the bad habits that you pick up in law school because you have to read opinions. Law is taught through the case method. In other words, to learn property, torts, or contracts, you read cases. Frankly, most of them are not well written. It didn't occur to me when I was in law school just how poorly written these opinions were.

So I think it's a combination of these things: inertia, poor models, bad habits, and lack of good training.

Eds: What single piece of advice would you give all lawyers to improve the clarity of their writing?

JK: I think it starts with attitude and an open mind. Lawyers have to stop thinking that the old ways are best. They have to stop copying old forms and aping old models. Then we can start to talk about technique. But if they don't realize that there is something wrong with most legal writing and they aren't open to changing their own style, of course all the technique in the world won't do any good. They have to care enough about it to want to change, and they have to inform themselves on how to go about changing by reading some books or taking a CLE course or finding a good editor.

Eds: That leads nicely to our next question. Focusing in on
      that lack of will that you mentioned, what can you do
      to motivate lawyers to want to write clearly, and to
      develop some of those skills?

JK: You can show them the empirical evidence I just
      mentioned — that their reader prefers plain language.
      It's strong evidence that I hope I've contributed to.
      If lawyers care about connecting with their readers,
      then they will write in plain language. That's part
      of the motivation. It's all part of being open-minded
      and willing to change. I don't know what could be a
      stronger motivator than knowing that if you write in
      plain language — in a clear style — you are much more
      likely to connect with your reader. I hope you would
      agree.

Eds: Absolutely! Joe, you've been teaching and writing
      about plain language for lawyers for over 20 years.
      What has changed in this time?

JK: Again, that's a hard one to answer because if there is
      change, it's incremental. But the one thing I've men-
      tioned that I think has changed significantly is the
      amount of time being devoted to legal writing in law
      school. This has been in response to pressure from
      practicing lawyers and the American Bar Association,
      who keep telling law schools that the young graduates
      aren't writing well. Of course, I sometimes wonder
      whether this isn't a universal complaint. Complain-
      ing about any kind of writing seems to be the national
      pastime. But it's especially important in law because,
      after all, lawyers write and speak for a living.

      So in response to the complaints that law schools have
      been hearing from practicing lawyers, they have tried
      to improve their legal-writing programs in the last 10
      or 15 years. And it's only moving more strongly in that
      direction. Whereas students used to take 3 or 4 credit

hours of writing, which isn't many out of, say, 90 credit hours to graduate, now it's more likely to be 6 and at some law schools even more. It probably averages only around 4 or 5, but the movement is in the direction of more legal-writing opportunities in law school.

Schools are also moving to better status for legal-writing teachers. That's always been an issue. A lot of times, they were on short-term contracts. At some schools the contracts weren't even renewable. The schools would say, "You can teach here for only two years or four years. Then you have to leave." This, of course, makes no sense. They wouldn't tell that to a torts teacher or a contracts teacher. Presumably, experience counts, and you tend to be a little better teacher as time goes on.

That is all changing too. Slowly, the status of legal-writing teachers — I should say professors — has improved. I'm lucky. At my law school, I'm on tenure track — always have been. As a matter of fact, our law school was the first one to put all its legal-writing teachers on tenure track and never change that. And this was in 1984 or 1985.

Eds: How does Barbara Child's notion that writers in all professions rely on "convention rather than thought" apply to legal writing?

JK: Lawyers rely on forms and formbooks. They have to write a lot of the same kinds of documents — wills, for instance, leases, and so on. And lawyers tend to turn to the formbooks because nobody ever showed them a better way.

Eds: Would you agree with Lee Clark Johns that we all rely, at least to a certain extent, on the sex life of the file cabinet?

JK: I suppose to some extent we do. This is the inertia factor that encourages lawyers to be unclear in their

writing. They just don't have the time or the inclina-
tion to change their forms. It's a tough hurdle to get
over, but I suggest starting with a form that they use
most often — for example, the standard will. With the
needed drive and the skill, they could spend a couple of
hours and improve it. Take it one form at a time. Now,
the lawyer's response might be, "Well, why should I?
My clients aren't demanding this." This is where we
need to add a little public pressure into the mix. I wish
there were some way to convince the public that legal
writing doesn't have to be unclear. If a client were to
say to the lawyer, "You've written this will for me, but
I can't read it. I don't understand what it means, and
it's really important to me who I'm leaving the Ponder-
osa to. If I'm paying for it, I think you ought to write
in a way I can understand!" That'll be the day, when
people speak up like this. Then my ship will come in.

Eds: Do you think that clients often expect that legal writing — no matter how obtuse — has to be that way?

JK: I think that's exactly right. The public has been conditioned to think that legal documents have to read that
way.

Eds: Like the Ten Commandments.

JK: Right, like they're set in stone and can't be changed.
Every chance I get, I try to paint a different picture:
legal documents don't have to be written in legalese.
At least the typical consumer documents (wills, leases,
loan contracts) ought to be understandable. People
ought to be able to understand what the document
says. Now, I don't know whether that message is getting through to the public.

Eds: You cite David Mellinkoff as saying that legal writing
is "wordy, unclear, pompous, and dull." On the cover
of *The Scribes Journal of Legal Writing*, you suggest
that legal writing is "turgid, obscure, and needlessly

dull." Aren't these characteristics of all ineffective professional writing, though?

JK: The short answer to that is yes. The great strength of Mellinkoff's study is that it was so scholarly. He reviewed the history of legal language going back centuries and debunked the age-old myths about the need for convoluted writing. Anyway, I think it's absolutely true that legal writing has all those characteristics you mentioned. I'm sure you can make the same complaint about a poor scholarly paper or a poor paper in any discipline.

Eds: You've written that clear writing is a goal we can all agree on. Just to play devil's advocate for a minute, don't we all sometimes deliberately choose to be unclear because we don't want the reader to understand us? Are lawyers particularly prone to do this?

JK: Those are interesting questions. Again, I don't think that most writers are deliberately obscure or write deliberately muddled prose. They do it unwittingly or through a lack of skill. I think it's a competence issue more than a conscious effort to obfuscate. They do it because they can't do any better. Here, we're talking about obscurity and muddled writing. I think that's a little different from being evasive.

It's also different from being vague. Vagueness is an idea I've spent some time thinking about. Legal writing especially relies on vague phrases: *reasonable doubt, due process of law, cruel and unusual punishment.* Those are very vague terms that lawyers argue about all the time. All language is vague at some point; even terms that you think aren't very vague can be vague.

Take the term *car*. You're walking down the street and say, "Well, that's a car. That isn't a car." And then you come upon something like the Chrysler PT Cruiser or

an SUV. Is that still a car? So one challenge for lawyers in drafting contracts, for instance, is vagueness:
how vague or specific to be. Sometimes they settle
for more vagueness because the parties can't agree on
something. "Okay, so this has to be done within 90
days." "Well, I don't know. That's too long. Let's just
say within a reasonable time but no longer than 90
days." I don't consider that to be muddled. I just see it
as a decision to use somewhat more vague language in
the document.

Muddled or turgid writing is also a little different from
ambiguity. I just finished helping to redraft the Federal Rules of Civil Procedure. These rules have been
around since 1937, and they govern the procedures in
all U.S. federal trial courts, the federal district courts.
Lawyers study them in law school and use them every
day, and yet when we tried to "restyle" them (a term
the committee used), we noticed all kinds of inconsistencies and ambiguities. This proved once again that
clear language is not imprecise. It's more precise than
traditional legal style.

Eds: I want to return here to the training that lawyers receive in writing. You mentioned that in the last 10 to
15 years there's been more of an emphasis on that, but
could you elaborate a little bit on just what kind of
training in writing lawyers receive either in law school
or before or after?

JK: I can't really speak about before, but I can speak about
in law school. Most courses or programs are structured like this: you'll have maybe two courses. The
first course will be devoted to writing legal memorandums, which is just another way of saying performing
legal analysis on paper. So law students have to do
some research, come up with some cases, and put them
in the form of a memorandum that analyzes the legal

issues and how this problem will be resolved. It's an objective legal memorandum. If a client walks into my office and gives me this set of facts, what am I going to tell the client? If I don't already know, I'm going to do the research, find the law on the subject, and write a memorandum so that I can advise the client or a supervising attorney can advise the client.

Then, typically, in the next course, law students move on to writing briefs — more persuasive kinds of documents. The brief argues the client's case for a trial court or appellate court. Although briefs are more persuasive, they still depend on legal analysis: you're trying to analyze not *how* the case is most likely going to turn out but *why* it should come out in your client's favor. It's more argumentative than the legal memorandum.

Where law schools have until recently fallen down is in teaching what we call "legal drafting." Legal drafting has to do with laying out rights and duties — writing contracts, writing statutes, administrative rules, or some kind of procedural rules. That's historically been the neglected area of legal writing. Again, though, more and more law schools are starting to require their students to at least get some training in drafting these types of dispositive legal documents.

So there are really three main types of legal writing: objective memorandum, persuasive brief, and the dispositive document like a contract, will, set of bylaws, or administrative rule. In the past, the emphasis has been very much on the first two. The legal memorandum is written for the lawyers in the office. The brief is written for the judge. But the contract, the will, the mortgage is typically written for the consumer or business client, and that's exactly where there has not been enough emphasis before in law school. When new lawyers graduated from law school without any training in legal drafting, they went to formbooks and copied the forms. Nothing ever changed. That's one reason why the public documents that the consumer saw were so bad. Now there's increasing emphasis on training lawyers in how to draft the documents that the consumer typically sees.

Eds: Although university students preparing to be lawyers get the writing training for their profession that you've just discussed, most students preparing for other professions don't get equivalent training for the writing they'll do in their professions. What are your thoughts on this?

JK: I'm surprised to hear that because I see only the people who are coming into law school; if that's true, it seems appalling to me. What professions don't require verbal skills?

Eds: I think very few professions have the kind of formalized training that yours does.

JK: You would know more about that than I do. It seems like a serious deficiency. When I hear that question, I think to myself, what professions don't require much writing? Medicine? I guess that seems right: most doctors don't do a lot of writing unless they're doing research of some kind. Nurses don't do much writing, I suppose. I don't know how much writing computer programmers do.

Eds: I think a lot of the professions do a lot of writing — they just don't get the training for it. I don't know of a lot of writing programs for nurses; they're offered by consultants. And I don't know whether in the nursing program there are courses for the writing they will have to do.

JK: I can't believe those professions aren't demanding that their graduates be skilled in writing.

Eds: Well, English Ph.D. programs don't have a lot of courses in how graduate students should write or teach, so I guess they're just things you're expected to figure out for yourself.

JK: That seems to me to be a seriously bad state of affairs.

Eds: What would you say is the most important thing that we should do to improve the general teaching of writing in colleges and universities?

JK: Well, I'm afraid this is going to be a predictable answer, but . . . teach the principles of clear writing and the importance of it. Because I've been working on legal writing for 20 years, I'm not as familiar as I might be with the general books that are out there, but aren't there a lot of good ones? I think of Sheridan Baker's *Practical Stylist*, Jacques Barzun's *Simple and Direct: A Rhetoric for Writers*, Richard Lanham's *Revising Prose*, John Trimble's *Writing with Style*. How about Joseph Williams's *Style: Ten Lessons in Clarity and Grace*? I learned a lot from that book. It's a great book. In fact, we in the Legal Writing Institute just gave him an award. We call it our Golden Pen Award.

There are resources out there, and I'm sure that you would know some other good ones. Assign those. And in business schools, bring to bear some of this empirical evidence that plain language connects with readers and saves businesses money. As far as literary tradition goes, plain language isn't baby talk and doesn't dumb down the language. I like to count Walt Whitman, Mark Twain, E. B. White, and lots of others in the plain-English tradition. I think plain English is the American idiom. Remember Whitman's line, "The art of art, the glory of expression, is simplicity. Nothing is better than simplicity."

Eds: How would you recommend that writing consultants help their clients make their writing clear?

JK: Read the books on plain writing. Know your stuff.
      Know what works.

      Consultants have other battles besides just knowing
      the techniques and guidelines for writing clearly. They
      have the challenge of getting the support they need
      when going into an organization. For consultants to
      be successful going into organizations or businesses,
      they need support from the top for whatever they're
      trying to accomplish, and they need to involve all the
      affected personnel in their work. It's not just a mat-
      ter of going in and giving a seminar, although that can
      be a good start. If they're going to change the way an
      organization writes, they need to have a long-term
      commitment. It would be nice if they could just go in,
      do a little training, administer some kind of objective
      test, and say, "Okay, you are all now good writers."
      But obviously, that's not the way it works. It takes
      cultural change to change the way an organization
      communicates — that and sustained effort over time.

Remarks on Accepting the 2010 Award from the Section on Legal Writing, Reasoning, and Research of the Association of American Law Schools

I'm proud today to belong to three groups, each one part of the next.

First, I'm proud to be a member of WMU–Cooley's Research & Writing Department, which after all nominated me for this award. One of our professors is here today — my dear friend Ann Wing, who (rumor has it) wrote the nominating letter. I haven't read it. Twenty-five years ago we *were* the Research & Writing Department, teaching four sections of 20 students each. Those numbers have gone down considerably since then.

Another Cooley prof is here today, Otto Stockmeyer, who teaches contracts but taught legal writing many moons ago. Otto hired me for my first job out of law school and later recommended me for the job at Cooley. Good call, Otto.

And I should mention Don LeDuc, Cooley's president and dean. Don has advocated forcefully for all of us over the years, as many of you know. If you don't, check out his remarks in Volume 8 of *The Journal of the Legal Writing Institute*.

So I'm pretty lucky to have landed at Cooley.

The second group I'm proud to belong to is one I share with you: I'm a legal-writing teacher.

Nobody in law school has a more important charge than we do — trying to fix a centuries-old affliction and teach

241

students how to write clearly, simply, directly. Think of the staggering waste and confusion and frustration caused by poor writing in the old style — not to mention the endless ridicule. Bryan Garner, just to pick a name [Garner was in the audience], says that we lawyers "have a history of wretched writing, a history that reinforces itself every time we open the lawbooks."[1] Legal-writing teachers stand between law students and the abyss. We're the ones charged with teaching the power, elegance, and — for the reader — joy of clarity and simplicity.

It's not easy. One of my favorite lines is from Jacques Barzun: "Simple English is no one's mother tongue. It has to be worked for."[2] And to teach plain writing, we have to overcome all the counterinfluences in law school — like, say, the old Federal Rules of Civil Procedure or the soon-to-be-old Federal Rules of Evidence. These are not models of clarity, people, but shaking them off is hard for some. I could tell you a bunch of stories. Have you ever seen photos of Abraham Lincoln before and after the Civil War? It's remarkable how much he aged during those four years. Likewise, when I began work on redrafting the civil rules in 2001, I was a young man. And look at me now.

And then imagine my dismay when, just last summer, the Standing Committee on Federal Rules — which deserves great credit for restyling projects — reinserted one single, solitary *shall* back into the civil rules, while admitting that the word is "inherently ambiguous." You'll find the whole story in Volume 12 of *The Scribes Journal of Legal Writing*.[3]

So I say that we have at once the hardest and the most important job in the legal academy. We teach writing — disciplined, tangible thinking. And you can't point to a group of law professors that spends more time with students, thinks more creatively about teaching methods, reads and marks up

---

[1]   Bryan A. Garner, *The Elements of Legal Style* 2 (2d ed. 2002).
[2]   Jacques Barzun, *Teacher in America* 48 (1945).
[3]   *See* this book at 92–93.

more student work, or engenders so much grumbling that turns into appreciation down the road.

Nor is there a group that works more collaboratively. I've learned so much from all of you, through the AALS section, and the Legal Writing Institute, and ALWD — all the programs, conferences, and publications. Think of the incredible array of resources and scholarship we've produced, along with the efforts we make to mentor new profs, share assignments, maintain two active listservs, produce a yearly survey, push for better status, recognize each other's accomplishments, and take legal-writing instruction worldwide.

I remember the early LWI conferences at Puget Sound, trying to soak up as much as I could and meeting Marjorie Rombauer, Mary Lawrence, Barbara Child, Ralph Brill, and others. I remember thinking, "Well, this is pretty cool; here I am hobnobbing with hall-of-famers."

But you know what? Everyone here deserves a plaque. And it should read: "To (your name here), who showed future lawyers how to make legal writing hang together, make it clear and telling, and make it plain."

Finally, the third group: I'm proud just to be a teacher — our most important professional class. It's the stuff of literature, deep memory, and inspiration. I'm sure you all know the line from Henry Adams: "A teacher affects eternity: he [or she] can never tell where his influence stops." Adams meant this in the sense of "for better or worse." But I'm pretty confident about the kind of influence we have.

Being a sentimental guy, I love the sentimental movie *Mr. Holland's Opus*. The ending just about does me in. Mr. Holland, a music teacher, has worked his whole career on a symphony. But he could never quite get it finished for production because he was busy teaching. (You may know the feeling.) Anyway, the school cuts the music program, and as he's leaving the school for the last time, he hears a commotion in the auditorium. He walks in, and there's the whole community, standing and applauding. One of his former students, now the governor, says, "It might be easy for him to think himself a failure, and he would be wrong. We are the melodies and the notes of your opus, Mr. Holland. We are the music of your life." Then the curtain opens to show many of his former students, waiting with their instruments. And he conducts his symphony.

The highest compliment that one person can pay another is this: "He was my teacher. She was my teacher." And to be honored by teachers — like you, my friends and colleagues — is an honor supreme.

Thanks, everybody.

Remarks on Accepting the 2015 John W. Reed Lawyer-Legacy Award from the State Bar of Michigan

This award "is presented periodically to an educator from a Michigan law school whose influence on lawyers has elevated the quality of legal practice in our state." I was nominated by two of my former students. Award winners had three minutes — strictly enforced — for their remarks, which were videotaped and presented at the State Bar's annual awards banquet.

I've tried all my life to avoid clichés, like "honored and humbled." I'm honored, of course, but recognition like this is not apt to make you feel humble — unless it's named after Professor Reed.

I've tried all my professional life to advocate and teach plain language — in its full sense of clear communication. Hence the books, the articles, my part in redrafting the Federal Rules of Civil Procedure and Federal Rules of Evidence, 30 years of meeting with students, and, of course, the Plain Language column in the *Bar Journal*.

I hope all this has elevated the quality of legal practice — not just because poor writing wastes everybody's time and money but also because of the public's dim view of legalese, our centuries-old curse. It diminishes respect for our profession.

I accept the award with a nod toward all teachers — everywhere. Teachers change lives forever. And a particular nod toward legal-writing teachers. Nobody spends more time with students, trying to teach them how to be coherent, and clear, and simple, and direct — that is, how to serve their readers.

I must thank WMU–Cooley Law School. Everything I have accomplished professionally, I owe to the opportunity that Cooley gave me decades ago.

Finally, my thanks to the State Bar for the Plain Language column. I'm proud of that little column and the influence it's had, really, around the world. Now in its 31st year. I doubt that any legal-writing column will ever match that.

But just to make sure, I have an announcement tonight: I'm not done. Not until I'm pronounced dead or daft.

Robert Frost, from his poem "Reluctance":

> Ah, when to the heart of man
>> Was it ever less than a treason
> To go with the drift of things,
>> To yield with a grace to reason,
> And bow and accept the end
>> Of a love or a season?

So please stay tuned. Please keep reading. Please, please write in plain language, for everyone's sake. And please accept my deep thanks for this award.

ACKNOWLEDGMENTS

The essays in this book first appeared in these publications:

- *You Think Lawyers Are Good Drafters?* — in the *Green Bag*.
- *You Think the Law Requires Legalese?* and *You Think Anybody Likes Legalese?* — online in *Legal Writing Editor*.
- *Guiding Principles for Restyling the Federal Rules of Civil Procedure* — with the package of restyled rules when they were distributed for public comment.
- *Lessons in Drafting from the New Federal Rules of Civil Procedure* and *A Study in Editing* — in *The Scribes Journal of Legal Writing*.
- *Wrong — Again — About Plain Language* — online in *The Legislative Lawyer*.
- *A Curious Criticism of Plain Language* — in *Legal Communication & Rhetoric: JALWD*.
- All others (except the interviews and remarks) — in the *Michigan Bar Journal*.

Index

Index

headings and subheadings
examples of, 81–83, 111–12, 129, 163
in Federal Rules of Civil Procedure, 24, 38–39, 80, 81–83
importance of, 38, 81, 163, 170–71
here-, *there-*, and *where-* words, 32–33, 93
herein, 17–18
hereof, 31, 93
heretofore, 33, 93
Hinkle, Robert, 97
However, 100, 170
How to Mangle Court Rules and Jury Instructions (Kimble), 16n, 93n, 221
How to Write Plain English (Flesch), 150n
How to Write Regulations and Other Legal Documents in Clear English (Redish), 150n
hyphens
aversion to, 222
with phrasal adjectives, 6, 164

in connection with, 6
in consideration of, 136
Indemnification: *Banish the Word! And Rebuild Your Indemnity Clause from Scratch* (Ammon), 18n
indemnify, 18
indents
hanging within subparts, 101
progressive for subparts, 25, 80, 101
initialisms, 164, 170
in its discretion, 107n, 109n
intensifiers, 26–27, 83–84, 100n, 138
inter alia, 165
Internal Revenue Code, poor model for law students, 3
International Plain Language Federation, 210n

introductions, in legal articles, 161
Issue-Framing: The Upshot of It All (Garner), 199n

jargon. *See* legalese
Johanson, Stanley M., 151n
Johns, Lee Clark, 233
John W. Reed Lawyer-Legacy Award, 245
jointly and severally, 18
judges
advice for writing judicial opinions, 219
preference for plain language, 153, 159–60, 208n, 229
resistance to footnoted citations, 190–91
Judges on Effective Writing (Garner), 208n
jury instructions, improving, 220–21

Keeton, Robert, 131
Kessler, Joan B., 159n
Kimble, Joseph, 15n, 16n, 19n, 58n, 73n, 86n, 93n, 134n, 138n, 142n, 147n, 148n, 149n, 150n, 152n, 153n, 160n, 165, 198n, 208n
award from AALS Section on Legal Writing, Reasoning, and Research, 241
background in plain language, 157, 225–26
drafting consultant for federal rules, 21, 35, 97, 106, 236, 245
editor, *The Scribes Journal of Legal Writing*, 222
John W. Reed Lawyer-Legacy Award, 245
legal-language survey (1978), 158–59
role in plain-language movement, 228–30
use of live grading, 157